LETS GO!

PUBLISH

Dedication

To my two best brothers,

Joseph A Kelly and Angel Edward J. Kelly, Jr.

Thank you for all of your support in my writing and publishing efforts.

You guys are always the best.

John Chrin v Matt Cartwright for Congress

Chrin has a unique approach to solving the big problems in America.

Running for office is a grueling, tiring, busy, and difficult process. There is always something to do. There is always someone who wants something from you. and did I say you are always tired. Yet, somehow, as a candidate, even on the bad days, you have to walk around with a smile on your face and a nice comment ready to come from your lips when you greet the next person.

Even if your purpose for running, like John Chrin's, is altruistic so you can help your city, state, or the country, and you really do not want to be a politician, just a worthy representative of the people, there are many who simply will not believe you. Good people like John Chrin endure the issues

So, here we are approaching the general election in 2018 and right now, I have the only idea in the world that actually solves the problem with illegal interlopers hiding in the shadows of the United States. Moreover, the winning Chrin platform has a unique approach to solving Obamacare, and the long-due needs of Senior Citizens as well as young Americans. The platform as you will see in this book, is designed with something good for everybody

The real concern many conservatives have is whether any political party is interested in a solution as Congresses of the past have been too content at having no solution as their solution. Democrats want everybody, including non-citizens to vote and before Trump, Republicans did not know what to do once they got power and so they were often disappointing. Isn't it great that Donald Trump is our President, and he is supporting John Chrin.

Americans want a country that is all-American with Americans in the driver's seat; and they want their guests to be invited to the table. No drop-in-guests from other countries allowed. You won't want to put this book down as you learn the ins & outs of the best solution possible for immigration, Obamacare, Social Security, and School Loans for our nation's young.

I am working hard so that John Chrin will not let you down on this outstanding platform. Thank you for reading this book.

BRIAN W. KELLY

Copyright © September 2018,   **Brian W. Kelly**
Title: How John Chrin Will Beat Matt Cartwright for Congress
Editor: **Brian P. Kelly**
Author   **Brian W. Kelly**
Sub Title: Using a u*nique approach to solving the big problems in America.*

Referenced Material: Standard Disclaimer: The information in this book has been obtained through personal and third-party observations, interviews, and copious research. Where unique information has been provided or extracted from other sources, those sources are acknowledged within the text of the book itself or in the References area in the front matter. Thus, there are no formal footnotes nor is there a bibliography section. Any picture that does not have a source was taken from various sites on the Internet with no credit attached. If resource owners would like credit in the next printing, please email publisher.

Published by: ....LETS GO PUBLISH!
Editor in Chief.. Brian P. Kelly
Email: ....info@letsgopublish.com
Web site..www.letsgopublish.com

Library of Congress Copyright Information Pending
Book Cover Design by **Brian W. Kelly**

Text Editor—Brian P. Kelly

ISBN Information: The International Standard Book Number (ISBN) is a unique machine-readable identification number, which marks any book unmistakably. The ISBN is the clear standard in the book industry. 159 countries and territories are officially ISBN members. The Official ISBN for this book is

978-1-947402-60-7

The price for this work is........... .... **$9.95 USD**

10	9	8	7	6	5	4	3	2	1

Release Date: .... September 2018

Acknowledgments

In every book that I write or edit, I publicly acknowledged all of the help that I have received from many sources. Some of these wonderful people are still on earth and others have made their way to heaven.

I would like to thank many people for helping me in this effort. I appreciate all the help that I received in putting this book together, along with the 177 other books from the past.

My printed acknowledgments were once so large that book readers needed to navigate too many pages to get to page one of the text. To permit me more flexibility, I put my acknowledgment list online at www.letsgopublish.com. The list of acknowledgments continues to grow. Believe it or not, it once cost about a dollar more to print each book.

Thank you all on the big list in the sky and God bless you all for your help.

Please check out www.letsgopublish.com to read the latest version of my heartfelt acknowledgments updated for this book. Thank you all!

In this book, I received some extra special help from many avid supporters of America including Dennis Grimes, Gerry Rodski, Angel Brent Evans, Wily Ky Eyely, Angel Irene McKeown Kelly, Angel Edward Joseph Kelly Sr., Angel Edward Joseph Kelly Jr., Ann Flannery, Angel James Flannery Sr., Mary Daniels, Bill Daniels, Angel Robert Garry Daniels, Angel Sarah Janice Daniels, Angel Punkie Daniels, Joe Kelly, Diane Kelly, Brian P. Kelly, Mike P. Kelly, Seamus McDuff, Katie P. Kelly, Angel Ben Kelly, and Budmund (Buddy) Arthur Kelly.

Preface

Here we are citizens in a truly exceptional country. Yet, even here in America all is not perfect. And, though this country as a whole is exceptional, individually, we are not necessarily exceptional. John Chrin recognizes that and is ready to help make Northeastern PA a better place to live.

Where did all the hate come from? It seems like it is just in the past few years that the odor of hate in America is strong enough (if you'll pardon me) to knock a buzzard off a "feces" wagon. To use a big word to describe it. It is *palpable*.

Can we do anything about it? Well, one thing is for sure, if *"we the people"* as a group do not smarten up, things will get a lot worse and they may never get better again. Somehow Americans have consistently been electing inferior representatives without doing the due diligence necessary to assure these knaves want to serve the people rather than serve themselves.

We have Democrats such as the new Democrat leader Maxine Waters who wants leftist thugs to bully conservatives in restaurants and public spaces. That is not going to help. John Chrin like most Americans wants an America in which the people practice the old Christian maxim "love thy neighbor." Chrin thinks we must stop the hate and get the work done for the people.

Chrin agrees that one of the best things that has happened recently in America is that God intervened and gave us all another chance. He sent his beloved Son over two thousand years ago and though that helped, just recently, God saw that things do not stay right in mankind for too many years at a time.

This time, he found a playboy rogue out in the fields of fun and prosperity in America and he let this rogue know that he had a big job for him. Donald Trump, who did not need God's job offer as life was treating him pretty good already, chose to accept the offer and he ran for President of the US and now he is here with us. We better not blow this opportunity to do the right thing for God. Stop the hate! Elect John Chrin as our representative in NEPA. John Chrin wants to help Donald Trump complete God's mission for America. Matt Cartwright is still on the Democrat hate team.

In this book, your author Brian Kelly takes a solid look at John Chrin and his normal campaign platform. To make Chrin and his mission to help Trump unstoppable, your author adds four new platform points to the Chrin agenda. These are big and powerful and helpful to seniors and young people alike.

They are explained in detail in Part II of this book. The platform points in Chapter 10 through Chapter 13 are the healing balm for a lot of ills that are plaguing our country right now. John Chrin is the type of leader to use these new ideas to solve a lot of big problems.

You are going to love this book since it is designed by an American for Americans. Few books are a must-read, but *John Chrin v Matt Cartwright for Congress* is a book you want to have, to read about the great methods Chrin may use to solve our problems.

The subtitle is *Chrin has a unique approach to solving the big problems in America* We expect that this short-run book will quickly appear at the top of the Area's most read list. If we do not gain back the greatness of our America, with the right people representing us, we may be again stuck with a knave such as Matt Cartwright and that means nothing good will happen for our area through another election cycle. Let's solve the problems now with Chrin, while we still have a great leader at the top of the country.

Sincerely,

Brian P. Kelly, Editor

Table of Contents

Chapter 1 Matt Cartwright Not Worthy to Serve Pennsylvanians.................1

Chapter 2 Who is John Chrin?...21

Chapter 3 Elect John Chrin as Your Representative for Northeastern PA 25

Chapter 4 John Chrin Wins Republican Primary for New PA District 8.......29

Chapter 5 It's Tough Being Unknown!.......................................31

Chapter 6 John Chrin for American Values 35

Chapter 7 Mr. Smith Goes to Washington...................................39

Chapter 8 John Chrin On the Issues 43

Part II Unique Platform Points **51**

Chapter 9 Intro & Brief Campaign Issue Overview.......................53

Chapter 10 Special Platform Points... The Preamble 59

Chapter 11 #1 Obamacare—One Line Repeal and Replace........................67

Chapter 12 #2 Illegal Immigration 69

Chapter 13 #3 Boost Social Security Now 75

Chapter 14 #4 Eliminate All Student Debt!!!...............................85

Other Books by Brian Kelly: (amazon.com, and Kindle) 97

About the Author / Editor

Putting this book together to help the Chrin election effort has been a big treat for me.

Brian W. Kelly retired as an Assistant Professor in the Business Information Technology (BIT) program at Marywood University, where he also served as the IBM i and Midrange Systems Technical Advisor to the IT Faculty. Kelly designed, developed, and taught many college and professional courses. He continues as a contributing technical editor to a number of IT industry magazines, including "The Four Hundred" and "Four Hundred Guru," published by IT Jungle.

Kelly is a former IBM Senior Systems Engineer and IBM Mid Atlantic Area Specialist. His specialty was designing applications for customers as well as implementing advanced IBM operating systems and software facilities on their machines.

He has an active information technology consultancy. He is the author of 177 books and numerous technical articles. Kelly has been a frequent speaker at COMMON, IBM conferences, and other technical conferences.

Brian was a candidate for US Congress himself from Pennsylvania in 2010 and he brings a lot of experience to his writing and editing endeavors.

Chapter 1 Matt Cartwright Not Worthy to Serve Pennsylvanians

When I asked him for help on an issue I had about some unfair business practices, he said, "No!"

It is a funny thing about politics and politicians. They promise a lot but do not deliver a lot. Matt Cartwright is a lawyer and a politician, so I guess we can say there is no saving grace there.

Consider this humorous scenario about politicians and terrorists to make a point. Terrorists take a group of politicians hostage. They ask for a ransom of $20 million and threaten to release one politician at a time if not given what they ask for. Let that one sink in. That's Matt Cartwright.

How about the all-time classic about lawyers. What is the difference between a dead skunk in the middle of the road and a dead lawyer in the middle of the road? Skid marks in front of the skunk.

Politicians gain much power after a term or two and it quickly becomes all consuming. That's why even good Congress persons often lose their fervor against term limits after their first term. They also learn where the money is and how they can keep their office and their jobs and make even more money. Look at some of the famous Congresspersons in the country such as Nancy Pelosi, Matt Cartwright's best bud, and if you want some really interesting information do some research about her wealth. As a politician Matt Cartwright is no Nancy Pelosi nor Hillary Clinton but they sure do like Matt an awful lot. He carries their water.

It may interest more than a few Democrats who think their politicians are not in the upper 1% of the wealthy. Nancy Pelosi makes 1% ers look like pikers. In her May 2015 financial-statements, she disclosed income that places her in the top one-tenth of the 1 percent of Americans. This may surprise many in light of the concern she's expressed about income equality and the distribution of wealth. Do as I say, not as I do. Tell me this. If all Congressmen make the same how do those in office making less than $200,000 per year wind up with a net worth well into the millions? Humph!

Who am I to say but DC politician Matt Cartwright often claims that Americans "deserve a congressman who doesn't make excuses but goes ahead and pays his taxes." Yet, Cartwright has failed to pay his own taxes on a luxury DC condo, resulting in thousands in penalties and late fees.

Worse than that? Matt Cartwright has joined forces with his liberal party boss, Nancy Pelosi, to support even higher taxes across the board. Americans deserve better than tax-raising hypocrite, Matt Cartwright.

Cartwright has no problem hurting his constituents

Tom Shepstone is a working stiff from Honesdale who after years of hard work eventually was able to run his own company. He calls it Shepstone Management Company, Inc. In a short book like this, I can't put in all of the missives that I know about, so I picked this one because Shepstone accuses Cartwright of playing his constituents for fools. That's us folks!

A lot of people in NEPA have made some money by owning drilling land in the right places and Pennsylvanians are paying less for natural gas while the US is a major world producer today because of fracking. Somehow that does not please Matt Cartwright and a number of other Democrats.

Here is a post Tom made on April 3, 2014 about Matt Cartwright.

Cong. Matt Cartwright has joined up with seven other like-minded members of the US House to urge EPA action on fracking, but is he serving his constituents or shilling for his former law firm?

Congressman Matt Cartwright of Pennsylvania's wildly gerrymandered 17th District chose April Fools Day to announce he and seven other House members were urging "EPA to address water contamination issues Pavillion, Wyoming; Dimock, Pennsylvania; and Parker County,

Texas." It was a bizarre action for several reasons and one is tempted to call Cartwright himself the butt of the April Fools joke, but that would overlook a more serious problem; the fact this serves the interest of his former trial lawyer firm, which has solicited lawsuits over fracking. It's no laughing matter.

Matt Cartwright the Trial Lawyer

Matt Cartwright is married to Marion Munley, of the Munley Law Firm in Scranton. The firm was previously known as Munley, Munley and Cartwright before Cartwright became Congressman Matt Cartwright. It ran this post on the law firm's blog, where it still appears (emphasis added):

Thursday, July 29th, 2010

EPA Wants to Regulate "Fracking" at Marcellus Shale

[Trump has relaxed many regulations of the Cartwright / Obama era.]

Previously exempt from government regulation, the drilling process called hydraulic fracturing or "fracking" may now be monitored by the Environmental Protection Agency (EPA). Fracking is a drilling technique used in the Marcellus Shale region using millions of gallons of water filled with toxic chemicals.

While the oil and gas industry stands by the safety of the process that has been used for years throughout the country, the EPA is undertaking a $1.9 million study to re-evaluate the process and to protect the publics' groundwater from pollution and depletion.

The regulation of fracking would repeal the 2005 exemption under the federal Safe Drinking Water Act.

If you are a property owner whose well has been contaminated or whose property has been damaged by well drilling, you may have a claim for damages against a drilling rig operator or the gas exploration company. The Marcellus Shale gas accident lawyers at Munley, Munley & Cartwright can advise you on your options. The attorneys at Munley, Munley & Cartwright represent victims who have been injured through no fault of their own. Contact us at 1-800-318-LAW1 or submit a free online claim evaluation.

The firm also continues to promote the idea suing gas companies might be a good idea with posts such as this one from last year (the substance of which is rebutted here by a wonderful example connected with one of the largest and most successful enterprises in Cartwright's own district).

So, who is Cartwright representing in his appeal to the EPA, which is an entirely superficial document that doesn't even make a specific request? It's obviously a show piece designed to reinforce the false ideas planted in his firms's own earlier lawsuit solicitation where he actually says fracking has been "exempt from government regulation."

What kind of fools did Matt Cartwright think his future constituents were when his firm issued that solicitation? Hydraulic fracturing and drilling are both subject to intense government regulation at the state level and Matt Cartwright isn't stupid. He knew that then and he knows it now. Indeed, his April Fools letter says this:

While we appreciate that states act as the major source of regulation for unconventional drilling operations, we believe the Environmental Protection Agency has a key role to play in oil and gas development. Despite the industry's exemptions from some of our bedrock environmental laws, the EPA does have the power to help ease the burden of directly impacted communities.

Who are we to believe–Congressman Matt Cartwright or Matt Cartwright the trial lawyer who was trying to gin up some fracking lawsuits? Or, is this simply a bone being thrown to one of the Congressman's special interest constituencies, which include not only his former law firm, where his wife still practices, but groups like the American Association for Justice, which represents trial lawyers all over the country?

Matt Cartwright: Deliberately Ignorant

Regardless of the purpose, it appears Congressman Matt Cartwright has chosen to maintain a degree of ignorance for purposes of promoting the idea fracking is dangerous or has contaminated water supplies. He cites three examples of his supposed concerns with fracking:

Pavillion, Wyoming, Dimock, Pennsylvania and Parker County, Texas have all experienced the negative impacts of an under regulated drilling industry first hand. Each community was grateful when the EPA stepped in to help deal with their water contamination issues, and disheartened when the EPA stopped their investigations, leaving them with polluted water and little explanation.

All three of these cases are, first of all, way outside the 17th Congressional District he represents. Secondly, once again, he knows full well what happened in each case because they have each received tons of publicity. The bottom line: there was no evidence in any of these cases to support a conclusion that fracking has contaminated water supplies. See here, here and here.

That's why the EPA withdrew from all three cases and why two successive EPA Administrators under his party's President Barack Obama as well as numerous other officials have declared it safe. And, Dimock? Really, Matt? How many times does do the state and EPA have to prove the water is safe before you'll accept it? "EPA testing of water wells found no regulated pollutants exceeding federal limits," as one Bloomberg reporter correctly observed. How many lawsuits have to collapse for lack of evidence before you believe?

This is where things get really foolish, however. Congressman Matt Cartwright serves parts of Carbon, Lackawanna, Luzerne, Monroe, Northampton and Schuylkill Counties.

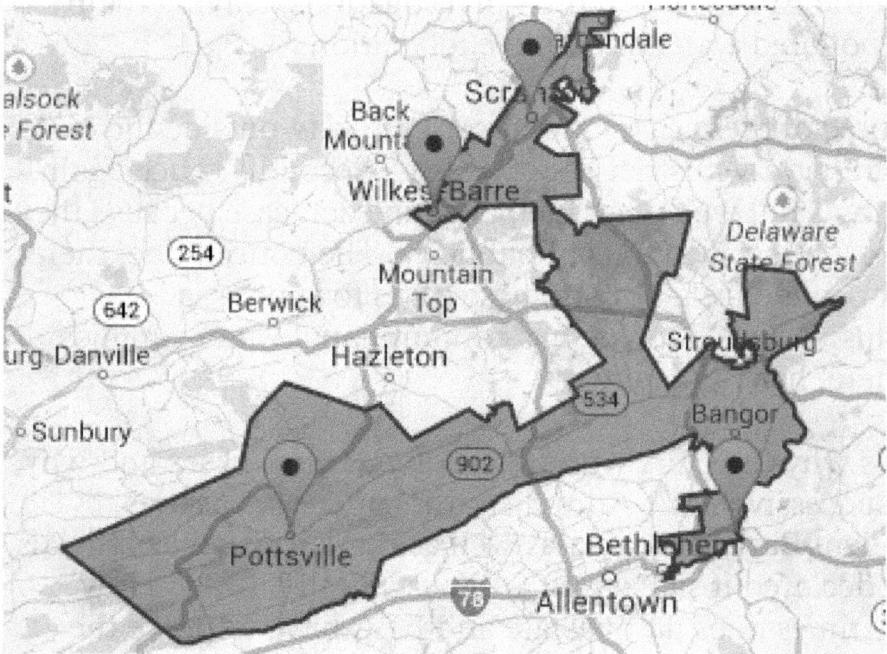

Crazy isn't it? Anyway, these six counties have received over $2 million of money from natural gas drilling, despite the fact there is no drilling or fracking of any consequence occurring in any part of Matt Cartwright's district. If you thought that mattered, well, the Congressman says the April Fools joke is on you.

Act 13 Impact Fees to Counties in 17th Congressional District

County	2011	2012
Luzerne	$ 272,267	$ 268,512
Lackawanna	$ 190,754	$ 185,933
Monroe	$ 144,094	$ 142,259
Carbon	$ 55,357	$ 54,560
Northampton	$ 252,599	$ 249,943
Schuylkill	$ 125,808	$ 123,527
Totals	$ 1,040,879	$ 1,024,734
2-year Total		$ 2,065,613

But, here's the rest of the story. Another specific project to be funded with natural gas development impact fees is the treatment of acid mine drainage from the Old Forge Borehole. The story is told in a superb Scranton Times article, excerpts of which follow:

Impact fees gathered from Marcellus Shale well operators will fund an effort to treat acid mine drainage from the Old Forge borehole.

At its board meeting Wednesday, the Commonwealth Finance Authority approved a $1 million grant from the Marcellus Legacy Fund, made up of a portion of impact fees gathered under Act 13, the authority's deputy press secretary Lyndsay Frank said.

The award will go to Susquehanna Mining Solutions LLC, an entity created in 2011 and based in Hanover Twp., according to business filing documents from the Pennsylvania Department of State.

Chris Gillis, a local inventor affiliated with the corporation, said he plans to acquire land in Duryea Borough and build a treatment facility that will eventually be able to treat the entire volume of water flowing from the borehole into the Lackawanna River…

The Old Forge borehole was drilled in 1962. Every day, it dumps between 60 million and 100 million gallons into the Lackawanna River, providing an outlet for water that pools in a coal mine void large enough to hold a volume comparable to Lake Wallenpaupack.

The borehole is clearly visible on Google Earth. Upstream, the Lackawanna River looks unremarkable. Downstream, it's orange, leaving a noticeable streak in the Susquehanna downstream of the two rivers' confluence. The borehole is the largest point source of pollution to the Chesapeake Bay.

Old Forge Borehole

There's more here and here, but what's Matt Cartwright think about this? Well, a search of his website for the word "borehole" yielded no results. He's apparently too worried about non-existent groundwater contamination from fracking to pay attention to how it's cleaning up one of the worst cases of water contamination in the history of his district. Maybe it has to do with his trial lawyer associates' desire to do some rainmaking of their own. Then again, maybe it's just his April Fools joke on his constituents.

Comment1 on post

Good job, Tom….and let's not forget how Cartwright champions himself as a little guy for the little guy despite his father, Alton S. Cartwright, being former chairman of the

board and chief executive officer of Canadian General
Electric Company Limited now known as GE Canada. It
was the Canadian counterpart of the American company
General Electric. The unit became General Electric C

Comment 2 on post

Cartwright would make a good Rip Van Cuomo lookalike.

Matt Cartwright: Works against President Trump's accomplishments

There is no Democrat who will deny that by definition Matt
Cartwright is against Donald Trump and like all Democrats
he is hoping Trump fails and Cartwright will work with
Pelosi and Watters to impeach him when given the word.

If Cartwright & company are successful here, the items in
the below list of Trump accomplishments are what
Americans will lose. Trump accomplished these in just 500
days of continual uphill battles such as Democrats like
Cartwright never lifting a finger to help him. Cartwright &
company when in power again can take them all away.

**500 DAYS: In his first 500 days in office, President
Donald J. Trump has achieved results domestically and
internationally for the American people.**

> ➢ Since taking office, President Trump has strengthened
> American leadership, security, prosperity, and
> accountability.

- ➤ After 500 days, the results are clear: the American economy is stronger, American workers are experiencing more opportunities, confidence is soaring, and business is booming.
- ➤ President Trump has re-asserted American leadership on the world stage, secured vital investments in our military, and stood up against threats to our national security.
- ➤ President Trump has put the American people first and made government more accountable.

AMERICA'S ECONOMY IS STRONGER: The American economy is stronger today and American workers are better off thanks to President Trump's pro-growth agenda.

- ➤ Nearly 3 million jobs have been created since President Trump took office.
- ➤ 304,000 manufacturing jobs have been created since President Trump took office, and manufacturing employment stands at its highest level since December 2008.
- ➤ 337,000 construction jobs have been created since President Trump took office, and construction employment stands at its highest level since June 2008.
- ➤ Under President Trump, the unemployment rate has dropped to 3.8, the lowest rate since April 2000, and job openings have reached 6.6 million, the highest level recorded.
- ➤ 67 percent of Americans believe now is a good time to find a quality job, according to Gallup.

➤ Only under President Trump have more than 50 percent of Americans believed it is a good time to find a quality job since Gallup began asking the question 17 years ago.

➤ President Trump prioritized job training and workforce development to empower workers to seize more opportunities, signing an Executive Order to expand apprenticeship opportunities.

➤ President Trump has restored confidence in the American economy, with confidence among both consumers and businesses reaching historic highs.

➤ Consumer confidence in current conditions has reached a 17-year high, according to the Conference Board.

➤ Optimism among manufacturers has hit record highs under President Trump, according to the National Association of Manufacturers.

➤ Small business optimism has sustained record-high levels under President Trump according to the National Federation of Independent Business.

➤ President Trump signed the historic Tax Cuts and Jobs Act into law, cutting taxes for American families and making American business more competitive.

➤ American families received $3.2 trillion in gross tax cuts and saw the child tax credit double.

➤ The top corporate tax rate was lowered from 35 percent to 21 percent so American businesses could be more competitive.

➤ President Trump has rolled back unnecessary job-killing regulations beyond expectations.

➤ In 2017, President Trump far exceeded his promise to eliminate regulations at a two-to-one ratio, issuing 22 deregulatory actions for every new regulatory action.

- The Administration rolled back rules and regulations harming farmers and energy producers, such as the Waters of the United States Rule and the Clean Power Plan.
- Regional and community banks and credit unions got relief after President Trump signed legislation reducing harmful requirements imposed by the Dodd-Frank Act.
- Since taking office, President Trump has advanced free, fair, and reciprocal trade deals that protect American workers, ending decades of destructive trade policies.
- Days after taking office, the President withdrew the United States from the Trans-Pacific Partnership negotiations and agreement.
- President Trump's Administration is working to defend American intellectual property from China's unfair practices through a range of actions.
- The President improved the KORUS trade agreement with the Republic of Korea, which will allow more U.S. automobile exports to South Korea with lower tariffs and increase U.S. pharmaceutical access to South Korea.
- American agriculture has gained access to new markets under President Trump.

AMERICA IS WINNING ON THE WORLD STAGE: President Trump has re-asserted American leadership on the world stage and is achieving results for the American people.

- President Trump followed through on his promise to move the U.S. Embassy in Israel to Jerusalem.

- President Trump ordered an end to United States participation in the horrible Iran deal and immediately began the process of re-imposing sanctions that had been lifted or waived.
- The President has taken action to confront aggression by Iran and its proxies.
- The Department of the Treasury has issued a range of sanctions targeting Iranian activities and entities, including the Islamic Revolutionary Guard Corps-Qods Force.
- Under President Trump, the United States has led an unprecedented global campaign to achieve the peaceful denuclearization of the Korean peninsula.
- President Trump's leadership has contributed to the return of 17 Americans held overseas.
- In May 2018 alone, Venezuela released one American and North Korea released three Americans who came home to the United States.
- The President has secured historic increases in defense funding in order to rebuild our Nation's military with the resources they need, after years of harmful sequester.
- President Trump signed legislation to provide $700 billion in defense spending for fiscal year (FY) 2018 and $716 billion for FY 2019.
- The United States has worked with international allies to decimate ISIS.
- President Trump ordered strikes against Syria in response to the regime's use of chemical weapons in April 2017 and April 2018.
- The Trump Administration has imposed a range of sanctions on the Maduro dictatorship in Venezuela, including sanctions targeting Maduro and other senior government officials.

- ➤ AMERICA'S COMMUNITIES ARE SAFER AND MORE SECURE: President Trump has worked to secure our borders, enforce our immigration laws, and protect the safety and security of American communities.
- ➤ Despite limited resources and obstruction from Congress, President Trump has worked to take control of our border and enforce our immigration laws.
- ➤ President Trump has called on Congress to provide the resources needed to secure our borders and close loopholes that prevent immigration laws from being fully enforced.
- ➤ President Trump authorized the deployment of the National Guard to help secure our borders.
- ➤ President Trump's Administration has carried out immigration enforcement efforts based on the rule of law.
- ➤ From the start of President Trump's Administration to the end of FY 2017, U.S. Immigration and Customs Enforcement (ICE) Enforcement and Removal Operations (ERO) made 110,568 arrests of illegal aliens.
- ➤ Arrests made in this timeframe represented a 42 percent increase from the same timeframe in FY 2016.
- ➤ Of the 110,568 arrests made, 92 percent had a criminal conviction, pending criminal charge, were an ICE fugitive, or had a reinstated final order of removal.
- ➤ President Trump has made clear that his Administration will continue to combat the threat of MS-13 in order to protect communities from the horrendous violence the gang has spread.
- ➤ In 2017, the Department of Justice worked with partners in Central America to file criminal charges against more than 4,000 members of MS-13.

➢ The Trump Administration has cracked down on the import and distribution of illegal drugs in order to stop them from reaching our communities and causing even more devastation.

➢ As of April 2018, U.S. Border Patrol has seized 284 pounds of fentanyl in FY 2018, already surpassing the total of 181 pounds seized in FY 2017.

➢ The President has launched a nationwide effort to fight the opioid crisis, which has devastated communities across America.

➢ The President's Opioid Initiative seeks to reduce drug demand, cut off the flow of illicit drugs, and save lives by expanding treatment opportunities.

➢ President Trump signed an omnibus spending bill which provides nearly $4 billion to address the opioid epidemic.

➢ The bill included $1 billion for grants focused on the hardest hit States and Tribes and provided funding for a public-private research partnership on pain and addiction.

AMERICA'S GOVERNMENT IS MORE ACCOUNTABLE: Since taking office, President Trump has worked to ensure government is more accountable to the American people.

➢ President Trump has confirmed the most circuit court judges of any President in their first year, and secured Justice Neil Gorsuch's confirmation to the United States Supreme Court.

➢ President Trump has signed legislation to bring more accountability to the Department of Veterans Affairs and provide our veterans with more choice in the care they receive.

➢ President Trump signed the Department of Veterans Affairs Accountability and Whistleblower Protection Act of 2017, improving processes for addressing misconduct.

➢ President Trump signed the VA Choice and Quality Employment Act into law, authorizing $2.1 billion in additional funds for the Veterans Choice Program.

➢ President Trump successfully eliminated the penalty for Obamacare's burdensome individual mandate.

➢ The President's Administration is seeking to provide more affordable health coverage and broader access to affordable alternatives to Obamacare plans.

➢ President Trump has released a blueprint to lower drug prices for Americans.

➢ President Trump has ensured that the religious liberties and conscience of Americans are protected and respected by the Federal government.

➢ President Trump signed an Executive Order to protect the free speech and religious liberties of groups such as the Little Sisters of the Poor.

➢ The Department of Justice issued guidance to all executive agencies on protecting religious liberty in federal programs.

Chapter 2 Who is John Chrin?

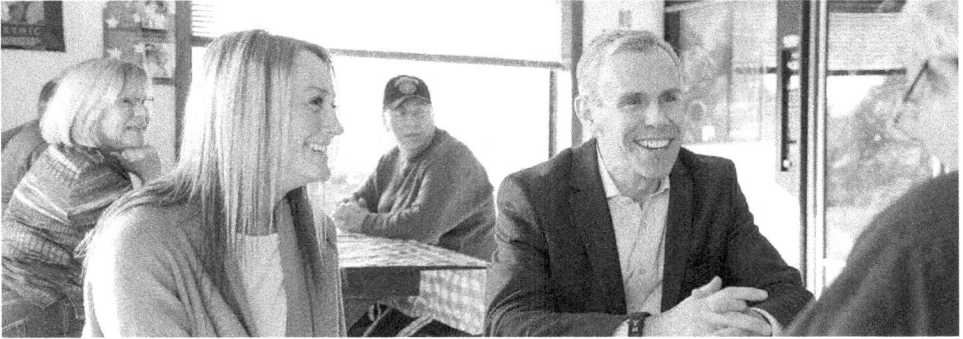

John would say that he is both nice and tough

A 10th generation Pennsylvanian, John R. Chrin was born at St. Luke's Hospital in Fountain Hill, Pennsylvania and raised in Easton. Today, he is a successful self-made businessman and Partner at Circle Wealth Management, LLC, an investment advisory firm founded by his wife, Maria Chrin.

Home for the first fourteen years of John's life was an apartment in Fountain Hill PA., until he moved to Palmer Township. His mother, who had John when she was 17, worked hard to support him and his brother. John credits her, his grandparents, and step-father for the strong values and work ethic which has been the foundation of his success. Education has also had a profound impact on his life.

It was at Fountain Hill Elementary, Broughal Middle School, and Easton Area High School where John found lifelong Pennsylvania mentors and teachers who encouraged and inspired him. His first job at age 12 was as a paperboy delivering the Bethlehem Globe-Times. He enjoyed it so much that he doubled up and added the morning delivery route for The Morning Call.

John was the first member of his family to attend college and paid his own way at Lehigh University with loans, scholarships, and summer/part-time jobs. One of those jobs was at Keystone Food Products, a snack manufacturer in Easton, where he experienced the positive impact of a local business on the community.

While working at Keystone, he became a member of the International Bakery and Confectionary Workers Union. During college, John also worked at Roadway in Tannersville and became a member of the Scranton Teamsters Union. In addition, he worked as busboy and dishwasher at the Minsi Trail Inn restaurant in Bethlehem.

John graduated with honors from Lehigh University with degrees in Economics and Industrial Engineering. He later attended Columbia University's Graduate School of Business, where he earned a Master in Business Administration with honors. It was at Lehigh that John met his wife Maria. They have been married for 30 years and have three children.

After Columbia, John began what would become a highly regarded career in banking where he earned praise for great achievement with the highest integrity. He rose through the ranks, during his twenty-year investment banking career, to become a Managing Director at JPMorgan Chase.

In 2009, John decided to make a change and share with young people the lessons learned during the financial crisis.

At the time, The New York Times described Chrin as the "rare investment banker who enjoyed keeping a low-profile." He returned to Lehigh, as the first Global Financial Services Executive-In-Residence, to teach business ethics and mergers & acquisitions in the University's College of Business and Economics.

After three years at Lehigh, John returned to the business world and joined Circle Wealth Management, an investment advisory firm founded in 2007 by his wife. Maria Chrin, a native of Honduras, had a successful 15-year career at Goldman Sachs prior to launching CWM. Its mission is to empower clients, 80% of which are women investors and their families, by helping them make sound financial and life decisions.

Based on his experience, John Chrin is a passionate believer in the economic power of education. He will strive to create affordable educational and training opportunities for students and adults in Northeast Pennsylvania and the Lehigh Valley.

Winning the competition for good jobs isn't just about degrees, it's about learning skills and gaining knowledge that help people succeed in the real world.

New job creation and stronger local economies are among his top priorities.

He believes that Members of Congress can and must play an active role in bringing economic development to their districts. In order to provide the right training programs and educational opportunities, there has to be an understanding of the needs of existing businesses and the skills which will attract new companies and industries to the region. John's first-hand experience with the best and worst of America's businesses and of the global financial system will be a driver of his stance on policies. He is a unique advocate for reforms, especially those related to the financial system, in that he understands what the real-world impact will be; whether laws will work as intended or make problems worse or potentially create new ones.

Knowing where John Chrin stands on most issues that matter for Northeastern Pennsylvanians, Brian Kelly, your author, had no second thoughts when he told his family and friends that Chrin is our guy and that finally with Matt Cartwright gone, good things can again come to the people in our home towns.

When we get a bit further in this Book of Chrin, in Part II, in a speech worthy of Lincoln Douglas debate credentials, John Chrin shows us all how to solve the issues of today that will have the most positive impact on the most Americans.

As you know, these issues include Obamacare, Social Security Cost of Living, Millennials and Student Loans, Resident Visas, and Paying illegal interlopers to go back to their home country saving American taxpayers over a half-trillion dollars each year. I expect that most Americans and most Pennsylvanians will love these unique solutions. No Congressman and no Senator in the US offers a platform as bold as this. Matt Cartwright could only dream about something so positive for America.

Chapter 3 Elect John Chrin as Your Representative for Northeastern PA

John Chrin and redistricting

Laura Olson of the Morning Call spoke with John Chrin, who is running for Congress in PA, about the redistricting that went on in Pennsylvania in February 2018. This is her report from the Morning Call.

Republican John Chrin will continue his bid to challenge Democratic U.S. Rep. Matt Cartwright in District 8, despite being drawn out of the congressional district in which he had been campaigning since May.

Chrin, who bought a home in Palmer Township in November after launching his campaign in the 17th District, now lives in the new 7th District under the state Supreme Court's revised district map.

Many people in PA are not happy with the mess the courts gave us as District Numbers are not something regular people are accustomed to having to relearn.

That congressional district (7th) includes Lehigh and Northampton counties and part of southern Monroe, and largely overlaps with the district that Republican U.S. Rep. Charlie Dent will be retiring from there at the end of the year.

By adding all of Northampton County into the 7th District, the city of Easton and several other parts of Northampton — including Palmer Township — were removed from Cartwright's former 17th District.

Now called the 8th District, Cartwright's seat was consolidated into the state's northeast corner. It includes Wayne, Pike and Lackawanna counties, and parts of Luzerne and Monroe counties. Chrin's objective of course is to unseat Cartwright and give the seat back to the people of Pennsylvania.

An so, District 8, the new District 8, is where Chrin will continue his bid for Congress, he announced Tuesday morning.

"Whether the lines shift and the district is called the 17th or 8th are out of my control," Chrin said in a statement.

"District lines may change but people don't," Chrin continued. "In November, I will offer Northeast Pennsylvanians a choice between an out-of-touch Washington politician and a successful, self-made businessman who can't be bought by special interests and is focused on bringing economic growth to the region."

Cartwright has represented the 17th District for three terms. He won by eight percentage points in 2016, while Republican Donald Trump topped Democrat Hillary Clinton there by 10 points. The new district boundaries shift the seat's geographic makeup, but appears to have a similar partisan breakdown, according to an analysis by the New York Times.

Chrin has made significant personal investments in the congressional race last year, loaning his campaign $700,000, according to reports filed with the Federal Election Commission. His campaign spokesman, Brock McCleary, says Chrin intends to move into the new district.

Chrin's announcement on which district he'll pursue came as congressional candidates were able to begin circulating petitions Tuesday March 20, to get their names on the May 15 primary ballot.

That process was delayed by two weeks due to the legal fight over the state's congressional district map, which the state Supreme Court threw out last month. The justices had unveiled a new set of district boundaries just last week.

Most of the facts in this report were submitted by

lolson@mcall.com

Chapter 4 John Chrin Wins Republican Primary for New PA District 8

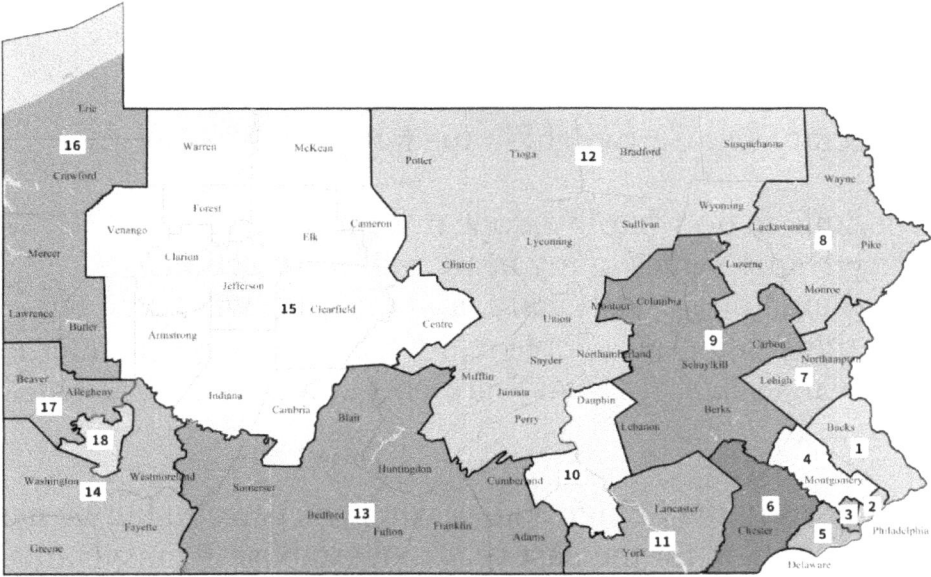

SCRANTON, Pa. -- John Chrin declared victory Tuesday in a tight race for the Republican nomination for the U.S. House in Pennsylvania's newly drawn 8th District. [Top right district shown on map]

The Republican candidate received an enthusiastic welcome from supporters at the Hilton in downtown Scranton. Chrin was running against two other Republicans, Joe Peters and Robert Kuniegel.

Peters, a well-known opponent with experience in both politics and law enforcement, had an early lead. Those numbers turned in Chrin's favor as more precincts reported results making Chrin the projected winner.

"What could be better? I mean, to be with such a great group of people, to be in Scranton, to now move on to what would be the third step to really try to the fight for the people of northeast Pennsylvania," Chrin said.

Chrin said he is looking forward to facing off against Democrat Matt Cartwright in the fall.

"Continue to do what I've done my entire life: live Pennsylvania values in my heart and in my actions, everything I do, to work hard, and the truth will come out, and I think when the people really see the difference in terms of the values in what Matt represents and what I represent," Chrin said.

Chrin lives in the Lehigh Valley where he is from, but he has only lived there for the past year to reestablish Pennsylvania residency in order to run in this race. Before then, he and his wife lived in New Jersey.

Chrin far outspent his opponents, even pumping an estimated $700,000 of his own money into his campaign.

Today, May 20, 2018, is also Chrin's 55th birthday. After he gave his victory speech, the crowd erupted into a rendition of "Happy Birthday."

Chapter 5 It's Tough Being Unknown!

"THE BIGGEST MISTAKE YOU COULD EVER MAKE IS BEING TOO AFRAID TO MAKE ONE."
~UNKNOWN

Everybody knows somebody sometime

It is typically not such a good thing when "everybody knows somebody sometime" and you are not on the list. When you are a guy who just returned to your roots, sometimes the press forgets that you are local. Sometimes, they root for somebody from Erie PA whom they may no better. Perhaps the other person married a local girl who has a pedigree with a family that runs a prominent local law firm—Munley & Munley. Those things happen. Everybody knows somebody sometime.

Some see that as a John Chrin obstacle in getting to know his constituency. His opponent has had a helping hand through marriage. Moreover, the law firm connections with the press have already brought in big advertising revenue

over the years. One might even say that because of Muney &
Munley, the local Scranton media may be characterized as
being in Matt Cartwright's hip pocket, so his "free" press
coverage is expected to be frequent and positive.

Being unknown has one major advantage for John Chrin,
however. It means that he is not Matt Cartwright, an out-of-
towner who has worn out his welcome in Northeastern PA.
Pennsylvanians know that Chrin is not Matt Cartwright, a
representative who has not done the job for PA constituents
during his six years...and it does not seem to bother him as
he is well loved by Maxine Watters, Nancy Pelosi, and of
course HRC.

For Chrin, when he says that he backs the President's
agenda, the people know he means it because it is true. For
the time Donald Trump has been in office, Cartwright has
backed the President zero times. Check out these contrasts.

The President is pro-life, Matt Cartwright's pro-life talk is
right-on, but his record is iffy. He says" he is pro-life. I don't
think so. The President wants a border wall. Matt
Cartwright is against it. The President wants a strong
immigration platform. Matt Cartwright goes the way Nancy
Pelosi tells him to go—no border wall. The President
lowered PA Taxpayers taxes. Matt Cartwright wants to raise
them. The President wants to give Seniors a big boost in
Social Security income. Matt Cartwright does not. There's
more. Check out the liberal Democratic Party platform and
you'll know where Cartwright stands on the issues.

The President wants to solve the student debt crisis and has
a plan to do so. Matt Cartwright has not signed on. The
President would like a Resident Visa Plan and a Pay-to-Go

plan to save about a $trillion on immigration costs that can be used for other programs. Matt Cartwright wants to keep funding illegal aliens; loves Sanctuary Cities and DACA. The President's stance is John Chrin's stance as Chrin knows that we can keep making America great. Matt Cartwright would like to reverse the gains the President has already made.

Matt Cartwright follows the Hillary Clinton agenda. The President nicknamed her Crooked Hillary. In August 2018 Hillary Rodham Clinton rewarded her buddy Matt Cartwright with an endorsement in his bid for re-election to Pennsylvania's 8th Congressional District. If Hillary wanted to endorse Chrin, he would refuse the endorsement because they have nothing in common.

John Chrin would say: "I fear that if I were to bring my unique platform points as revealed in the text of the speech that is in Part II, to Matt Cartwright's attention, they are so powerful, he would adopt them as part of his platform and it would make him feel unbeatable. However, in reality, Cartwright would not have the guts to implement such a bold platform for all Americans."

As much as John Chrin, your author, and those that check them out, want these platform points adopted for the good of America, having Matt Cartwright back in office hurting the Trump agenda as a Congressman from the 8th District would be too high a price for any Pennsylvanian to pay— even if Cartwright adopted what may be called the Chrin unique platform points as discussed in Part II of this book.

Many of Chrin's friends ask how he can hope to become known by people who live in any of the sixty-seven counties

that make up Pennsylvania. Well, first of all it helps to recall
that he is from Pennsylvania, born and raised, and secondly,
District 8 has just five counties and he knows were each of
them are because he has been there plenty of times. He will
be there throughout the campaign and afterwards, to meet
all the folks he can.

Unfortunately for those candidates that opponents call
"unknown," the priority of the management of media outlets
is to maintain their viability by bringing in ad revenue and
not giving up space or time to citizen candidates such as
John Chrin. So, I do know that it will not be smooth sailing,
for Chrin but he is up to the task. He will be there all the
time in all five counties. Feel free to use the Donate Button
on his web site to give him a boost in getting rid of the
Washington SWAMP candidate who lives in Moosic.

Chapter 6 John Chrin for American Values

We Are
REPUBLICAN
Because...

We believe the strength of the nation lies with the individual and that each person's dignity, freedom, ability and responsibility must be honored

We Believe in equal rights, equal justice and equal opportunity for all, regardless of race, creed, sex, age or disability.

We believe free enterprise and encouraging individual initiative have brought this nation opportunity, economic growth, and prosperity.

We believe government must practice fiscal responsibility and allow individuals to keep more of the money they earn.

We believe the proper role of government is to provide for the people only those critical functions that cannot be performed by individuals or private organizations and that the best government is that which governs least.

We believe the most effective, responsible and responsive government is the government closest to the people.

We believe Americans must retain the principles that made us strong while developing new and innovative ideas to meet the challenges of changing times.

We believe Americans value and preserve our national strength and pride while working to extend peace, freedom and human rights throughout the world.

Finally, we believe the Republican Party is the best vehicle for translating these ideas into positive and successful principles of government.

No man is an island

More and more Democrats from Pennsylvania such as my sister-in-law Diane, became or are becoming Republicans so they can be part of the big red wave that is making America great again. A vote for Matt Cartwright will not get us there. The list on the first page of this chapter is a great set of American values to remember. They are the values of John Chrin.

John Chrin is pro-life, and he is against selling baby parts and live brains, though some legislators such as say, Matt Cartwright, the incumbent in the 8th district by favoring Planned Parenthood over babies has forgotten this. Deep down most Americans are pro-life. Who wants to kill babies when they are the most vulnerable—before they have even gotten to make their first goo or gaw?

I do not believe in protecting smelts and bugs and protozoa if it causes harm to human beings. God made human beings with dominion over all life, and though we must be just caretakers of this awesome responsibility, it should not mean that humans must starve or be cold or freeze in the wintertime to please somebody's twisted environmental agenda. John Chrin supports Donald Trump's EPA and does not want the US to return to the days when turtle eggs were more important than yet-to-be born children.

In many ways some of the lofty ambitions of the Democratic Party leaders to create an equal world where there is no injustice has placed human beings per se in the back seat and has elevated non-humans to a status not intended by God

Moreover, with 7.44 billion people in the world, it is impractical for Americans to get jobs to support them all when they come to America and take our jobs. You know that at least half of the 7.44 billion would come here if we sent them an invitation or we were an open borders country.

People in Northeastern PA grew up with coal stoves and coal furnaces to provide heat and cooking in our homes. Coal served us well. Cartwright is against coal as are all Democrats. What good is it to freeze in the winter simply because an EPA regulation says coal is banned.

The coal stoves in my living room and kitchen did its job when I was growing up and it did the same in my wife's home. We are still healthy. Plus, we (the USA) have plenty of coal for the rest of the world. Why shut off the spigot? Why? It makes no sense. China is killing us economically using coal! We export coal to China. What do they know that we do not?

Don't you think that protecting unborn babies is more important than protecting anything else in life? Who is not pro baby? I think the big shot elite leaders of the Democratic Party have begun to endorse philosophies that give government, rather than God, supreme power. God rules supreme above all else, but Democrats like Matt Cartwright have forgotten that. When was the last time you were at a deathbed and heard the grieving family praying to the government?

Though recently I have come to like the philosophies of populists and conservatives like President Donald Trump, Ben Carson and Ted Cruz. I am not for communists such as Bernie Sanders nor for wannabe communists such as Hillary

Clinton. Why did Hillary endorse Matt Cartwright? Communists have failed everywhere.

There is no good choice on the Democrat side. Their platform is anti-American and anti-white and anti-baby. Matt Cartwright is a Democrat player and does not care about you. He wants a good spot in the Democratic Party and so he aligns himself with Nancy Pelosi and Chuck Schumer, and Maxine Watters, not John Q. Public.

Like the Republican nominees, John Chrin does not believe that corporations were meant to dominate individuals. Chrin also thinks that American corporations have an obligation in exchange for the privilege of operating in America to care for their employees and to help do everything in their power to protect and create American Jobs. We all know that our President feels the same way and we know John Chrin will help him with his pro-America agenda when we give Chrin our vote.

Hiring illegal aliens must be verboten!

Republicans and many rich Democrats even prominent Democrats such as John Kerry and the Heinz Company have no problem taking jobs overseas. Additionally, they have no problem trying to reduce the American wage to as low as possible by bringing in illegal foreign workers to force the wages down.

Democrats do not want to enforce our immigration laws. They see a huge voter pool in those who are to be granted amnesty. I am like John Chrin—for safe and secure borders and I believe in an America for Americans. If foreigners can live legally within our borders according to our laws, I am for that also. But, American citizens, that's us folks, must come first instead of last.

Chapter 7 Mr. Smith Goes to Washington

Jimmy Stewart from the movie, Mr. Smith Goes to Washington can be thought of as a guiding light for the Chrin campaign. The people like Jimmy Stewart and the honest guys like Jefferson Smith are indispensable for a great democracy / republic.

Mr. Smith Goes to Washington

Ladies and Gentlemen, I would like to present myself. My name is Jefferson Smith and I am going to Washington—if you select me of course.

Jimmy Stewart is one of your author's favorite actors of all time. He is as Americana as it gets with the perfect touch of honesty that makes even men admire the actor and the character the actor is playing. My favorite movie of all time is "It's A Wonderful Life." It gets me every time. Remember the big pot of cash the neighbors brought in to George Bailey, so he could keep the Building and Loan going. Well, that's how I think America should be. Don't you? Every hard-working American deserves a break.

What George Bailey did not need was the government stealing from his neighbors so that he could go to college and to heck with Pottersville. Well, it would have been Pottersville if George had not stayed to help all the people in Bedford Falls with his dad's Building and Loan Company.

Government intervention creates Pottersvilles and good neighbors create the likes of Bedford Falls. Let's let good people be good people again rather than taking so much from them that Mr. Potter, who acts like a leader of today's Democratic Party is the only one left with any money. John Chrin is a George Baily in our midst and I hate to say it in public; but Matt Cartwright is our very own Henry F. Potter.

Mr. Smith Goes to Washington exudes the same emotion from the viewer as *It's a Wonderful Life!* It was another of Frank Capra's big hits and Jimmy Stewart as Jefferson Smith is as down to earth as George Bailey. I can see John Chrin beating all odds and doing as good a job for Northeastern PA as Jefferson Smith did for his constituency. I know he will work his darndest to help Northeastern PA and America.

John Chrin is running for Congress to help fight the same type of corruption that Smith faced when he went to Washington. He is up to the task and he is ready to fight to make America, America again. With Trump as President, he will have a great man to help.

There is nothing separating Chrin from his chance to be our combination George Bailey and Jefferson Smith other than the coming general election. That's where you come in. For the sake of our state and country, I sure hope you choose to vote in John Chrin as our representative for NEPA. He'll do a great job for us—that is for sure.

Chrin's last name is quite uncommon. Unlike a name like Kelly, the name of your author, which is the second most common family name in Ireland (after Murphy), Chrin is not on many common name lists. So, he cannot ask you to think of him me as a Smith or a Jones. However, I know he would be pleased to serve you, the fine folks in NEP as the first Chrin you may know. John told me (Kelly) that he can't wait to meet you.

And so, will you indulge me please as I say again on behalf of John Chrin, my name is Mr. Smith, and I am going to Washington. I can't get there without your help.

Think of the corrupt conditions that existed in this famous movie as Mr. Smith, played by Jimmy Stewart. was little more than a bumpkin, when he first went into the Washington swamp of iniquity. But, like John Chrin, he was tough of character.

Smith was the naive and idealistic Jefferson Smith, the leader of the Boy Rangers. In Washington, Smith soon discovered many of the shortcomings of the political process as his earnest goal of a national boys' camp led him to a conflict with his state's corrupt political boss, Jim Taylor.

Taylor first tries to corrupt Smith and then later attempts to destroy Smith through a made-up scandal. Smith conducts a filibuster and finally sways everybody to pass the Boy Rangers Bill. It was heartwarming and to the point.

Please remember when you vote that John Chrin thinks like Jefferson Smith. Get the CD for the movie when you can and expect that it will make your eyes go moist. Chrin hops to be like Mr. Smith if he is selected. And, so, he asks all of you reading this short book to send him to Washington to serve in the United States House of Representatives. He would be a great choice. It'st time for Matt Cartwright to work at home.

Chrin hopes that when you send him to help Trump clean out the rest of the SWAMP. He has one more wish about this election and that is that when he checks in to his assigned seat in the HOUSE, there are approximately 434 additional like-thinking Representatives sworn in on Inauguration Day January 2019.

I want to thank you all again for reading this book and considering John Chrin, a fine man, to be your Congressman in the 8th District of Pennsylvania. Thank you very much.

Chapter 8 John Chrin On the Issues

John Chrin is very optimistic

Before I go over John Chrin's unique platform points in Part II of this book, with a humdinger of a speech, printed is five chapters, to help you better know who he is, I would like to share his opinion on the issues.

On Abortion
  ✓ A big against

On Budget & Economy
  ✓ For tax cuts

On Civil Rights
  ✓ Believe in equality

On Corporations
  ✓ For the common man

On Crime
- ✓ For the police over the criminals

On Drugs
- ✓ Against legalization

On Education (School Choice)
- ✓ Does not like government interference

On Energy & Oil
- ✓ Did not support Obama not using America's resources wisely
- ✓ Global warming is bogus.

On Environment
- ✓ Priority on people -- humans

On Families & Children
- ✓ Family man not for things Rush would call Feminazis

On Foreign Policy
- ✓ America First

On Free Trade
- ✓ For the good of America

On Government Reform
- ✓ Congress should not exempt itself from laws.

On Gun Control
- ✓ No
- ✓ 2nd Amendment is the key

On Homeland Security
- ✓ ICE is important.
- ✓ America First

On Immigration
- ✓ Legal immigrants OK but limited

On Jobs
- ✓ Tax cuts are right for America
- ✓ Pro Trump second round of cuts

On Principles & Values
- ✓ Conservatives.
- ✓ Obama not good for America
- ✓ School prayer is a good idea

On Social Security
- ✓ Check the platform in the speech in next chapter

On Tax Reform
- ✓ JFK believed in tax cuts to stimulate economy.
- ✓ Tax fairness is simple: Give the people money back.

On War & Peace
- ✓ For Peace through strength

Welfare & Poverty
- ✓ Help for helpless people
- ✓ Do not create helpless people

CHRIN NOTES ON ISSUES

John Chrin's principles are built on the premise that our government must do its part to ensure that the American Dream is achievable for current and future generations. This is a critical time in America's history. If we are to protect the American Dream and the values that make this nation great, we will need new leadership at the local level and bold ideas. I can tell you now, John Chrin is your best choice for the job.

ECONOMY & JOBS

Drawing on his experience as a successful businessman, John Chrin is enthusiastic about the economic opportunities for Northeast Pennsylvania. Nestled between the high-tax states of New York and New Jersey, Northeast Pennsylvania is uniquely positioned to harness its assets and capitalize on the businesses fleeing high costs of living. Northeast Pennsylvania offers a dedicated and talented workforce for employers. But we need a plan for success:

- The decline of manufacturing and industry jobs in our area makes it a necessity to provide retraining programs for individuals who need additional skills to succeed in the workforce.
- We should provide incentives for businesses of all sizes to offer apprenticeships to young people. Entrepreneurs training the next generation of small business owners, without the heavy burden of student debt.

- John Chrin will work to promote plans that strengthen our economy, increase worker pay, and cut taxes for the middle class and small businesses.

EDUCATION

As a product of public schools in Northeast PA, John Chrin feels strongly that public education is not living up to its potential in our country.

- We should reassess curriculums so that K-12 students have the technical, quantitative, writing, and speaking skills to succeed in the workforce.
- Public schools should have a financial literacy requirement so that students are prepared to face the financial challenges of young adulthood.
- Pennsylvania currently has the highest average student loan debt per borrower of any state in the nation. We need a plan to reassess student loans to lower the burden of pursuing college or vocational school.

IMMIGRATION

America's immigration system is broken because enforcement has been lax. We need to secure our borders by building the wall first, not only as a critical matter of national security but to also prevent illegal immigrants and contraband like drugs from flowing into our country. John Chrin strongly opposes sanctuary cities which flagrantly disregard the rule of law, are an insult to legal immigrants and hinder the collaborative efforts of state and local law enforcement and our federal agencies. You will see that the unique immigration plans in Part II eliminate sanctuary cities and DACA because they solve the underlying problem of illegal residents. Please make sure you check that out.

SECOND AMENDMENT

John Chrin is a strong supporter of the Second Amendment and a lifetime member of the NRA. John understands the importance of gun rights when it comes to self-defense, hunting, and home protection. These rights were enshrined in our Constitution because they are essential to our liberty.

HEALTH CARE

Obamacare is not working. It has failed in providing affordable, quality coverage and is driving up rates for everyone. John Chrin supports a health care system that puts patients first, allows small businesses to pool together to purchase plans, allows for the purchase of health insurance across state lines, and encourages competition.

I support healthcare coverage for individuals with pre-existing conditions.

I will protect and preserve the benefits of Social Security and Medicare promised to our seniors and all individuals who have paid into the system. We have an obligation to make the system solvent and make it stronger for future generations. Check out the plan in the next chapter.

PRO-LIFE
John Chrin is pro-life and will protect the sanctity of life.

Part II Unique Platform Points

Part II Objective

The objective of Part II is to provide a cluster of chapters that together provide Pennsylvania constituents an understanding of the issues resolved by the highly unique platform points that are revealed herein. After this introduction to Part II, five chapters follow with the final four chapters providing the unique platform points that will win the candidate the election and will help PA constituents as well as all Americans immeasurably

An outline of the chapter sequence in Part II is as follows:

- Chapter 9 Introduction and brief campaign issue overview

- Chapter 10 Preamble (A generic speech for the candidate to consider)

- Chapter 11 Obamacare One Line Repeal and Replace.

- Chapter 12 Illegal Immigration. Solve the problem for those living in the shadows, who want to live in America or for those who would prefer to be paid to go back to the home country.

- Chapter 13 Social Security's Cost-of-Living Fraud— Boost Social Security Now!

- Chapter 14 Student Debt Crisis—Wipe Out All Student Debt Now!

Chapter 9 Intro & Brief Campaign Issue Overview

We have reached the point in the book where the reader will have a difficult time knowing what is coming next. Your author Brian Kelly has provided his research to the candidate and it is now being presented in this format for the very first time ever so that all the people of Pennsylvania can read it.

For years Kelly has written book after book about how to improve America. He has written 177 books in total. The information in this book has previously been submitted to various Republican Campaigns such as that of John Chrin and Lou Barletta with the hope that they can use the information and the presentation style to convince the rest of Congress to take the action outlined in the specific platform point chapters. You may not be overwhelmed but you will not say, when you are introduced to all that we need to solve so many important American issues: "Is that all there is?"

As a result of discussions prior to this book being ready, the candidate has been provided with solutions in the form of four unique platform points and major descriptors to add to his full set of campaign platform points as discussed in Part II.

With this newly completed platform, I believe that all the great seniors as well as the young and other constituencies addressed in the four platform points can expect a lot of good things when they elect John Chrin to the United States House of Representatives to represent District 8 of our great State of Pennsylvania.

While John Chrin is working to capture PA District 8, Lou Barletta is working on his Senate campaign,. John Chrin has become familiar with the platform points discussed in this part of the book, from his team's conversations with your author.

For both John Chrin in the House and Lou Barletta in the US Senate, your author has a similar objective and a side hope that they will work together through the platform points presented for the benefit of all residents in our area, the State of Pennsylvania and the USA.

Many senior citizens such as myself and members of my family including one in particular, who graduated #3 at King's College have been hearing the unscrupulous Democrat attack ads about Republicans cutting senior benefits. Like most Democrat positions, these assertions are lies. The Democrats create a lot of fake news including the recent allegations against Judge Kavanaugh. Decent people cannot stand the rips Democrats keep trying to put in our Constitution.

Some hints re: discussion about Seniors in Chapter 13

I have studied the issue of seniors losing their homes because their SSR benefits have not kept up with inflation and it is appalling. The recommendations in the platform points will stop this from happening in the future.

Moreover, we know that too many some seniors are intimidated into paying their property taxes rather than buying nutritious food for meals, Democrats such as Matt Cartwright have enabled fraudulent cost of living estimates to reduce senior's benefits. They advocate deceptive methods such as the chained-CPI and the CPI-W. For the last thirty years, these have been used to cheat seniors of the opportunity to break even with inflation. Technically, they have been used to low-ball the SSR COLA calculations. The plan recommended for John Chrin and Lou Barletta eliminates this fraud.

You may or may not know that both the chained CPI and CPI-W and a few other methods, which have been the basis for the SSR COLA for seniors has been adjusted downward for years to the detriment of all seniors in the US. I am convinced that John Chrin in the House and Lou Barletta in the Senate will solve this problem using a plan similar to that presented in Chapter 13.

A normal human being unfamiliar with government hijinks designed to hurt seniors in their attempts to live healthy lives would ask, "Why not just use the actual inflation rate instead of the mumbo jumbo from the demented minds of coffee breath college professors?" The question begs to be answered. The recommendation in Part II is for John Chrin and Lou Barletta to change course and make things much better for seniors.

How did it get this way? We will tell you more in Chapter 13 but think of a bunch of heavy-bearded, light-minded, coffee-breath academicians advising the Democrat Party to stiff seniors on the inflation rate. I know this for a fact because for well over twenty-years, I was on the faculty as a peer professor at Marywood University, and Misericordia University. It's worse than you would think.

As you proceed through Part II and through the end of the book, you will see that Brian Kelly has written a preamble for John Chrin in Chapter 10 to precede the recommended platform points that solve this problem 100%. It is must-reading to set the stage for the day that Mr. Chrin can announce the changes he would propose along with a number of other great platform points.

The first part in Chapter 10 is the preamble and the second part, which is shown in Chapters 11 through 14, provide the specific platform points and a lot of other pertinent information to strengthen the arguments presented.

I have sent an earlier version of the entire speech to Candidate Chrin and Candidate Barletta. They can alay your fears and show you a much better way for Congress to really take care of senior citizens. I am sure you will like it as your annual SSR increment on a yearly basis will come in at a much more realistic number than the 2% received in 2018. How does 11% v 2% sound? The Chrin/ Barletta recommendation is even better than that. It makes seniors whole again.

John Chrin is working for all Americans

Soon you will read The Preamble in Chapter 10 to the platform points speech that I am encouraging John Chrin to deliver at a convenient venue in PA District 8.

The Preamble presented in Chapter 10 is designed to get constituent juices flowing as it offers help for everybody to know what this election is all about. It contains a generic introduction to the platform points and is designed to be delivered with the major points. You will see that it rolls right into the platform points, which I am convinced are meaty enough that they will carry the election for our soon-to-be-Congressman John Chrin, from District 8 in PA.

I hope you all enjoy reading The Preamble in the next chapter and the entire speech with all four major platform points presented in the final four chapter. If you feel like screaming and shouting "finally!" as you read this, feel free.

Chapter 10 Special Platform Points... The Preamble

Here it is: Preamble: John Chrin Suggested Speech:

Fellow Citizens,

Language is inadequate to express my gratitude for the privilege of submitting before you my candidacy to represent the fine people of Northeastern Pennsylvania as your Congressional Representative for District 8.

I would also like to thank you for the fine welcome, which you all have extended to me on this occasion. As I look out in my mind's eye, I see a vast sea of human faces who share a common interest, as do I, about the greatest questions of our times. Beyond occasionally agitating the mind, they now dominate the concerns of all Pennsylvanians and U.S. citizens, underlying the foundations of our free institutions.

Let us all make sure that freedom never becomes just another word for nothing left to lose.

The reaction to my U.S. Congressional candidacy by the people of Pennsylvania has been quite heartening. We have a president whose interest quite simply is to "Make America Great Again." By contrast, the embedded establishment and liberal leftovers in the SWAMP, have no interest in performing what is good for our country.

They are doing their best to undermine our president, without any repercussions, aided and abetted by a corrupt media, instead of building bridges to work for the good of all Americans, especially Americans from Northeastern PA.

It is no longer acceptable for a Democrat or a Republican to be a Never-Trumper. He is our president. Donald Trump is our president and his platform is my platform and when elected, I hope the extras in the platform that I introduce in this speech, become part of the Trump platform.

We all know that "Never-Trumpers" will never hold office again. Democrats such as Matt Cartwright, John Chrin's opponent, simply adore the establishment's impediments to the president's agenda along with a media whose interests are as adverse to the American people as the British press was during Colonial Times.

The Democrats and the Republican Never-Trumpers in the Senate, House, the federal bureaucracy and the degenerate mainstream press have done everything they could possibly do to thwart the will of 62,979,636 people who voted to clean out the SWAMP in 2016 with a fresh new presidential administration.

The legendarily venal Hillary Clinton lost the election after the public saw through her charade; yet she continues to parade around the world blaming everything from her own adoring fans at The New York Times, to white women like her, to the DNC, and probably even the cows in Wisconsin, a state she famously lost after taking it so for granted, she never visited.

She even blames the FBI and it never occurs to anyone that the best way to avoid an untimely FBI intervention in a political campaign is to not run for president while under federal criminal investigation. And all the while, Representative Cartwright stood by submissively, applauding, brownnosing, and enabling this farce of a candidacy. Why? For what good reason? Was it for her August 2018 endorsement?

It is time for the country to move on. Hillary lost, now get over it. We've had six years of Cartwright and that's about as much as any man or woman in America can take. For Cartwright; it's time to go. Maybe he'll even pay his taxes before he departs.

I am running for Congress to reclaim this seat which rightfully belongs to the people, not the extrinsic interests controlling our politicians, who would tear the Constitution in half without hesitation if it would please their donors and cheerleaders in the mainstream media. Despite the shameless lack of virtue that defines the top echelons of our government, our country itself is replete with honest citizens who would be humbled to work on behalf of their fellow countrymen and women. That is why I am running for the

US Congress against one of the biggest icons of mainstream mediocrity and corruption, Mr. Matt Cartwright.

Cartwright caters only to the whining anti-Trump crowd who are under the control of Maxine Watters. Watters is having a renaissance nationally with her "damn Republicans wherever you see them," rhetoric. She now thinks she can turn every trivial post on Facebook into a new Cuban Missile Crisis.

Despite the voters in even his home state rejecting the rank duplicity of former Secretary Clinton and her bleak vision of hopelessness and sovereign state decline, Congressman Cartwright never lifted a finger to help the people who support our president. He cannot add or he would know that we outnumber the opposition right here in Pennsylvania. But to him-- that's Matt Cartwright, folks; we do not even exist.

Though I, John Chrin, have a similar PA background to him other than I had to go for a real job interview to get my law position, as you know, Matt Cartwright simply came home with his girlfriend for the holidays to pick up his job offer as a gift from the Munley family.

The Matt Cartwright that we all see on TV claims that I am an out of towner. Yet, he would still be living in Erie Pennsylvania if he did not get a position in a law firm with the name Munley & Munley and now, Cartwright.

A local girl named Munley married him, brought him to Scranton and introduced him to dad so he did not have to stand the rigorous law interviews many others without connections persevered over the years. Why he thinks I,

John Chrin, am the carpetbagger here is certainly befuddling. Cartwright needs to consult with the man in the glass.

Even Cartwright's friends know that this do-nothing Congressman would prefer to turn the US into a globalist abyss rather than support its sovereignty or its people's dignity. Meanwhile, our great president is trying to find everybody a high-paying job by making it easier to conduct business in our country. I intend to help President Trump protect us from such parasitic interests. What are Matt Cartwright's intentions? Does he even care?

If there is one principle most cherished in all free governments, it is that which asserts the exclusive right of a free people to form and adopt their own fundamental laws, to manage and regulate their own internal affairs and domestic institutions. That is under constant attack by Mr. Cartwright and his legions of Clinton dead-enders.

Electing representatives of the people is not a triviality, but rather the expression of the most fundamental right of self-government. Without it, of course, this great United States would be like any other country in the world. It would not be the exceptional republic, which we the people have enjoyed since our own Declaration of Independence.

To say that I am honored to be here today presenting my candidacy for the House of Representatives, would be the understatement of the ages. Thank you for your reception and hospitality. I assure you that if elected, I will provide Pennsylvania and the United States of America the best representation in the US Congress of which I am capable. You can be sure of that.

End of Platform Preamble

Intro to Platform Points Chapters

We have many issues today of which the people are concerned. The idea in this discussion is to limit the topics to just four of the most prominent. I have asked John Chrin and Lou Barletta when they become our Congressman D8 and Senator respectively to adopt in full measure the points brought forth in the next four chapters by sponsoring legislation and informing the public of their support for the items discussed below.

The address contained in the next set of chapters uniquely addresses each of the four platform points as no other candidate for any US office has ever been able to do. I hope you will find the elements of this platform a welcome refreshment and inclusive of precepts that we all embrace and recognize as sincere and necessary for seniors as well as most other citizens of Pennsylvania.

The author's format in fashioning these arguments for adoption is to present each issue by area of concern and then offer the specific solution, which is part of the unique platform as promised. The issues and solutions will be presented one by one in the four major areas presented. I encourage you to read and digest all of the brannigans as presented without too quickly deserting any one major topical area.

Even if you are familiar with these points, the solution to each point is unique and the arguments are designed to win the people to the side of the candidates--both John Chrin and Lou Barletta, and other Republicans, so that the candidates will feel the support of the people when they bring forward the necessary legislation.

#1—Obamacare One Line Repeal and Replace.

#2—Illegal Immigration. Solve the problem for those living in the shadows, who want to live in America or for those who would prefer to be paid to go back to the home country.

#3—Social Security's Cost-of-Living Fraud – Boost Social Security Now!

#4—Student Debt Crisis Wipe Out All Student Debt Now!

Your author is asking candidates to put forth legislation when elected to help address all four issues as well as to provide full support for the other platform points as outlined in Chapter 8 as well as the overall Trump agenda.

The two opponents who are fighting Chrin and Barletta are Representative Matt Cartwright and Senator Bob Casey Jr. Both have been in office for at least six years (time to go!). For all of these years, they have been voting against all of the standard points in the Trump agenda and neither has indicated that he will miraculously decide by November to back the Trump agenda.

Over the next four chapters, let's discuss the four-major points above first--one by one, starting with Obamacare.

Chapter 11 #1 Obamacare—One Line Repeal and Replace.

This is going to hurt

OBAMACARE

Much to the chagrin of working Americans, Obamacare is still one of their top issues. They expect those whom they elect to solve this problem once and for all.

Thus, the first problem on the list is #1 because over 54% of Americans say that the availability and affordability of healthcare is their #1 issue. Despite Obama's empty promises from the past, many of us cannot keep our favorite doctors nor can we retain an affordable health plan that meets our needs.

The costs have been so prohibitive that many Americans have forestalled doctor's visits with often grave consequences. We all know that despite the remedy that Matt Cartwright and Robert Casey Jr. will again offer you, they know that Obamacare is a disaster.

However, they are enriched by the Federal Government to have a healthcare plan independent of Obamacare. So, neither has to care about you. Congress is not subject to the same laws as the citizens thanks to long-time Congressmen such as Cartwright and Casey.

My solution to Obamacare begins with clarity and definitive purpose. We start with a one-line repeal. The Obamacare beast is then vanquished and has no legal right to ever reappear. Following the repeal, we envision a plethora of competing less expensive alternatives provided by the marketplace without current tyrannical government controls.

Yes, folks, it really is that easy

Chapter 12 #2 Illegal Immigration

There are two solutions in this one platform point to solve illegal immigration. The two points are as follows:

1. Resident Visa Plan
2. Pay to Go

In February 2004, the late Arizona Senator John McCain recognized via Border Patrol reports that nearly four million people crossed our borders "illegally" each year following the big Reagan amnesty in 1986. Nonetheless, the fraudulent press insists that the total count of illegal immigrants residing in the United States is stagnant at eleven million, a mathematical impossibility if Border Patrol figures are to be believed.

Using John McCain's estimates with a rate of 4 million per year since 1986, the year of the Reagan amnesty, (1986 through 2018 equals 33 years) Thirty three years times 4 million per year equals 132 million interlopers today living in America. A better estimate is that the number is more like 60 million but theoretically, it can be as high as 132 million.

And these millions of foreigners, (60 million) most using fake ID's, receive full welfare benefits while, contrary to popular mythology, very few actually work in agriculture.

You may know that in September, 2018, the generally accepted estimates of the "experts were called into question by a Yale University Study. put the population of illegal foreign nationals (aka undocumented immigrants) in the United States at approximately 11.3 million. However, a new study by Yale, using mathematical modeling on a range of demographic and immigration operations data, shows that the actual undocumented immigrant population is more than 22 million and perhaps as many as 30 million. Though that is more like it, it is still a lowball estimate based on the facts.

There are in fact as many as 60 million and perhaps even more than that illegal foreign nationals living in the United States today. Nobody really knows but 60 million is a good number. While some individuals in this group may contribute to our society, on balance this is outweighed by the group's overall negative effect on US resources, whether they are drained by government assistance, lost employment opportunities for American citizens, or criminal offenses.

It is amazing how effective the fake-ID business is in turning illegal aliens into fake citizens who are thus enabled to enjoy American rights and privileges.

According to the 2011 GAO report entitled "Criminal Alien Statistics," the cost of crimes by illegal foreign nationals is $8.1 billion per year, and that's without even considering the incomprehensibly larger emotional toll this takes on families whose priceless loved ones can never be replaced.

If elected, I, John Chrin will introduce two pieces of legislation that will solve this problem of illegal residents in the shadows once and for all. Besides many other benefits, it stands to save the U.S. over $1 Trillion per year in addition to a major reduction in crime. The two solutions are known as *pay-to-go* and *the resident visa program*. Let's look at them now so that we all can understand how they solve the problem of illegal residents permanently.

Pay-to-Go

Most Americans are unaware that it costs taxpayers $30,000 per year on the average, per illegal alien in America to provide them with welfare benefits that would make them pleased. Each illegal resident and their dependent children, who sign up for Pay to Go, on the way back to the home country, will receive a one-time $20,000 stipend plus the individual expense back to the home country.

With a cost of $30,000 per year to support unwelcome interlopers, the taxpayer savings begin year one and continue at $30,000 per year per person forever. Not a bad deal for Americans and a great deal for aliens.

The program therefore quietly accommodates family reunification in the home country. A family of five for example, could do quite well back home after receiving $100,000 in stipends from Uncle Sam. Reuniting families in their own countries is a good idea for them and for America. The savings in welfare for Pat-toGo means there is no cost in year one and in year 2 and every year hence, the savings equal $30,000 for each person who "goes" back home, never to return.

Moreover, there is no settling issue as the returnee to the home country knows how to live there and does not create an issue for their home country of record. e

Resident Visa

Those illegal interlopers, who do not want to leave the US, have another option. They can sign up, be vetted, and eventually be approved for a *Resident Visa*. The visa will cost $200.00 to cover vetting in year one and for well-behaved holders of the Resident Visa, it will be renewable every year thereafter for a $100.00 renewal fee It is thus not permanent and there is no guarantee that a visa holder who misbehaves can stay in America.

To get a Resident Visa, a former interloper would agree to all stipulations after registering. At the end of the registration process, US officials would know where every former illegal interloper is living. The guessing about how many there actually are would be over and nobody would live in the shadows. There are a lot of beneficial features to this temporary Visa.

Stipulations would include full initial vetting; onsite renewal vetting; keep existing jobs; new jobs for Americans first; no voting; no citizenship; no welfare and no freebies of any kind. Everybody who applies (registers) is not automatically approved. After vetting, those not approved for the resident visa program may use the Pay-to-Go program to aid in their relocation back to their home countries where they are known by all their friends.

As the program would by definition entail 100% participation from illegal residents, estimates are as high as $500 billion per year cost savings in total for those who choose to go or for those who choose to stay using the no-welfare resident visa. Another $500 billion will be reclaimed over time for the lost wages of Americans accepting lower-wage jobs. Additionally, if we can figure a way for countries to reclaim their criminals, there is another $8.1 billion to be recovered.

Once the program is in effect, there would be no more illegal aliens in the country. Everybody would be legal. Resident visa holders would be legal and so there would be no shadows. There would be no need for DACA and no need for Sanctuary cities Let me repeat that. All issues with DACA would be over and Sanctuary Cities would be a thing of the past because there would be no shadows and no illegal interlopers.

Two additional programs are the part of my platform that I would now like to introduce in Chapters 12 and 13. Like the resident alien plans, no other candidate for public office

includes these great programs in their platform. You are
going to love these.

These two new programs offer the promise of a positive
effect on the health of the economy and both will contribute
to improving life for American citizens of all ages to live
well in this country. The first is about offering Social
Security recipients increased benefits to make up for
fraudulent cost of living increases based on an intentionally
fraudulent consumer price index perpetrated upon seniors
for the past thirty years. The second platform point is about
wiping out all student debt and the second. These are
presented in Chapter 13 and Chapter 14.

Chapter 13 #3 Boost Social Security Now

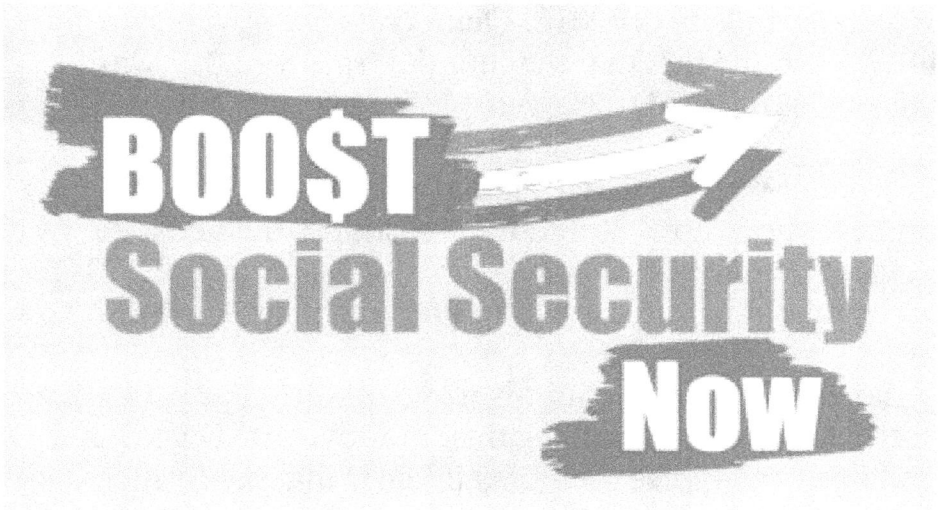

Social Security is taboo because Democrats such as Matt Cartwright no longer care about seniors. It is no longer publicly discussed by our duplicitous media despite the fact that seniors' issues need the spotlight now more than ever. Of course every Democratic candidate is using the time-tested liars playbook.

This is the Party that was throwing Granny off the cliff just a few years ago. They are the party that funded the Ku Klux Klan but they lie about it. Now, they simply point at their candidate's opponent and they say that he wants to lower Social Security. Only a fool would want to do that, but Democrats know that play has worked in every election because Democratic voters deep down want to believe the lie.

The Democrat-controlled media thinks seniors are greedy. They all in unison derided the implied greed of SSR recipients who received a whopping two percent cost of living raise to kick off 2018. Democrats are obviously oblivious to the fact that the inflation rate for 2017 was really 11%. It was not 2%, but 11%.

No wonder seniors are struggling when their cost for purchases goes up 11% and their cost of living boost (COLA) to make up for that is a mere 2%. These are 2017 cost of living figures. How do I know that, and you don't?

By the way, if Obama had his way with the chained CPI, a contrivance he supported against his advisors' wishes, it would be even worse. Seniors all know that the former president gave zero cost increases to seniors five times during his presidency showing all Democrats' lack-of-concern for seniors.

In 2014, the president pushed hard for advancing a surreptitious reduction of Social Security benefits by using the fraudulent chained-CPI mechanism. Obama's dubious market calculations would have cost retirees more than 2 percent of their incomes. Chained-CPI is a Democrat innovation. Yet, today all Democrats are blaming the chained CPI on Republicans. That of course is a lie but try to get a Democrat to believe that it is not true.

There are several ways senior Americans can investigate how much government lies cost them each year. The government purposely underestimates the cost of living using CPI-W or chained CPI to deprive the elderly of a commensurate actual increase in earned benefits. One such method for you to use to know your actual personal loss to government fraud each year is to subscribe to the Chapwood index or you may explore Shadowstats.com. There is proof-a-plenty.

Seniors unfortunately are running out of whatever financial cushion they may ever have had, and their plight today is dire. I encourage you all to research the degree to which government deceptions are resulting in these surreptitious deprivations.

After decades of Americans being saturated by our mainstream propaganda rags, it is refreshing to finally see the truth in print. The Chapwood Index reflects the true cost-of-living increase in America. It is updated and released twice a year. There the ruses or mis-directions of the government are not included in its pages. Instead, it truthfully reports the unadjusted actual cost and price fluctuation of the top 500 items on which Americans spend their after-tax dollars in the 50 largest cities in the nation.

It exposes why middle-class Americans—salaried workers who are given routine pay hikes and retirees who depend on annual increases in their corporate pension and / or Social Security payments (SSR)—cannot maintain their standard of living. Plainly and simply, the Index shows that their income can't keep up with their expenses and it explains why they increasingly have to turn to the government for entitlements for supplementation. It's either that or the proverbial poorhouse.

Mainstream Democrats such as Nancy Pelosi, Matt Cartwright, and Bob Casey Jr. exacerbate the situation by allowing the use of even more inequitable methods such as the new chained CPI. These mutations to the real cost of living figures help assure that seniors can languish in poverty as soon as possible.

The problem of lacking transparency on true costs (true inflation) occurs because salary and benefit increases are pegged to the fraudulent Consumer Price Index (CPI), which for more than a century has purported to reflect the fluctuation in prices for a typical "basket of goods" in American cities — but which actually hasn't done so for the last 30 years.

The middle class has seen its purchasing power decline dramatically in the last three decades, forcing more and more people to seek entitlements when their savings are gone. And as long as pay raises and benefit increases are tied to a false CPI, this trend will continue.

In the past, nobody was anxious to throw the proverbial grandma under the bus. Now, believe it or not, hordes of constituencies are lining up to be the first to fleece what should belong to her, into the eternal abyss, never to be seen again. The list of offenders includes: Congress, government officials, professors in academia, the "greatest" economic advisors the world has ever known, and dejected stand-alone economists who failed to gain tenure at a university.

This group of elite misfits have formed a diabolical consortium to cheat seniors out of their due cost of living increases promised from the very day the SSR act was passed in 1935 by Franklin Delano Roosevelt. Roosevelt promised benefits would be delivered in constant dollars but Democrats since Roosevelt have lied to the public.

As the mainstream Democrats kowtow to cultural elites and financial institutions, turning their backs on the workers and middle-class that defined their constituency for much of the 20th century, it is up to us to pick up the slack and fight for the rights of everyday Americans.

John Chrin is on the side of seniors in this battle. Matt Cartwright is on the side of the elites which includes lawyers such as his former law firm. Ask Chrin's mom if Social Security is important. She knows. Lou Barletta, who is running against Senator Bob Casey Jr. (a senator not rooting for seniors), is also a mainstay on the Pennsylvania pro-senior team.

It is important to repeat that when SSR was enacted, the president (Roosevelt) promised full dollar value throughout the years in order to ensure its passage in 1933. We cannot let this be undermined by the likes of Congressman Cartwright, Senator Casey and his allies under the command of Chuck Schumer and Nancy Pelosi.

Many Americans are concerned that the Social Security program itself may not be able to sustain itself while others see the government cheating on the cost of living increases (CPI) thereby predetermining a life of squalor for seniors.

All successful societies throughout the ages, have maintained respect and dignity for their elders. Not only is cheating seniors a moral failure, it is a sign of a civilization entering an era of decay.

While seniors are losing their homes and many, for want of bread and milk, are on the verge of heading to the proverbial poorhouse or worse—the clutches of the Grim Reaper,

Congress in 2018 pretended to care, giving a 2% raise. But then as unreported by the Democrat controlled media, they quickly snatched it right back in the dead of night via a Medicare Part B premium increase. This additional Medicare Part B charge for necessary health services for seniors was excluded from the cost of living calculations. How could Congress have missed that? Ask Matt Cartwright. It was intentional.

Thus, to pay Medicare part B, seniors have been forced to use their "generous" 2% raises, rather than to offset the costs brought forth from inflation in 2017 for which the 2% was intended. Since the real inflationary cost increases were closer to 11% according to the index, that means that instead of 9% that seniors were to endure, they accrued a full load of 11% in price increases. It's easy to understand why this constant drainage of resources is unsustainable for a senior citizen. More and more are forced to go to welfare or give up as their life-long homes are foreclosed.

How did we reach this point?

Early in the administration of disgraced former President Bill Clinton, an economist named Michael Boskin, along with Alan Greenspan, Chairman of the Board of Governors of the Federal Reserve System, devised a scheme that would allow for market basket "substitutions" to artificially lower the cost of living and result in lower payments to our oldest Americans.

These guys found value in having senior citizens help save big government money. Prior to their involvement, the consumer price index (CPI) was measured using the cost of a fixed basket of goods, a fairly simple and straightforward concept.

The identical basket of goods would be priced at prevailing market costs for each period, and the period-to-period change in the cost of that market basket represented the rate of inflation in terms of maintaining a constant standard of living. That was self-evidently fair and reasonable, and predictably resulted in seniors receiving annual COLA increases in tandem with the prices of goods actually increasing.

But Boskin and Alan Greenspan argued that when one item in the basket, for instance steak, became too expensive, the consumer would naturally substitute an affordable protein item such as hamburger for the steak, and that the inflation measure should reflect the costs tied to buying hamburger rather than the steak.

Eventually, it became OK for the bureaucrats to replace hamburger with less expensive tuna and eventually because the protein value was the same, cat tuna replaced regular tuna in the market basket.

The Bureaucrats like to tell observers that seniors did not have to eat the cat tuna, but their basket costs would be reflected the same if they did.

In simple terms, the government began to play tricks with Social Security annual inflation adjustments. It was intentional. To further obscure the true cost of living, other items were selectively removed from the basket when the prices were high and then reinserted when the prices were low again. The objective was to save the government money not to make sure that things were fair for elderly Americans.

Many people have been familiar with this ruse. For example, an economic commentator named Barry Ritholtz joked that Greenspan's core inflation metric can more accurately be described as "inflation ex-inflation," meaning inflation after all of the inflation has been excluded.

This demonstrates that the deception of seniors has been intentional, and it continues with a new notion called the chained CPI that will cost seniors even more. We need Chrin, Barletta, and Trump to get this back on track.

The fact is that government has deceitfully stolen directly from the pockets of our beloved seniors by denying them a fair cost of living increase just to stay even. Some have even suggested that the government believes a natural limit exists so they won't get caught in their ruse. They think they will get no criticism because over time, many of the complainants will be silenced by their deaths when they can no longer afford to pay up. Charming thought?

Walter J. Williams, an American blessing who operates the Shadowstats site has demonstrated that seniors have been stiffed by much more than just 125% and in fact should be receiving more than 4 times what their dollars were worth in 1980. That's $450 instead of $100.00.

Any senior would love to have even a small proportion of that loss back. Government lies cost seniors $350.00 on the hundred since 1980. But nobody will ever see that and great representatives, other than John Chrin and Lou Barletta from PA will not even tell Americans what is actually happening.

I hope I have convinced you all that seniors have been ripped off and are being ripped off financially all the time by their own government. Congress is the real culprit.

So, what do I recommend for now? First of all send senior-cheating Congressman Matt Cartwright home for good. He voted for six years in favor of those who stiffed seniors to the point of their giving up on life. Secondly, send Bob Casey Jr. home for the same reason. Both of these anti-American, anti-senior representatives ought to be begging for our forgiveness. They won't so let's send in the well-qualified replacement players – John Chrin and Lou Barletta.

Yes, please, in their stead, please vote for John Chrin and Lou Barletta.

I have asked John Chrin and Lou Barletta to take the following brief pledge to help seniors in NEPA.

I, John Chrin, [I, Lou Barletta] am pledging today to solve this fraudulent accounting for seniors cost of living increases as soon as I can. I am ready to take action by working to provide seniors with the COLA suggestions in this chapter for the next four years.

A gradual remedy for seniors, since it would be difficult to give seniors the proper increase immediately needed to offset this total quagmire caused by government malfeasance, your author's recommendation would be to approach it gradually, in a way that seniors would be somewhat pleased, and be able to live out their golden years in a much more dignified manner. Who can argue with that?

For the next four years, the COLA boost that I would strongly recommend, rather than be 0% to 2%, would be 15% above the real inflation rate as calculated by the Chapwood Index. This will help get seniors back a nice piece of their due.

After four consecutive years, that should be sufficient to remove seniors from the on-deck circle which they currently occupy directly outside the homeless shelter. That's all it would take. Then we can use the measurements that were in effect before the government fraud, in which a dollar was a dollar and a dime was a dime, and the US would have to vow to never stiff seniors again.

Thank you, dear readers, for your attention on these important matters.

In conclusion, I must again express my gratitude for your consideration and any support as we work together to make America even greater.

John Chrin and Lou Barletts need all the ehelp you can give to avoid a slimy Democrat determining what happens to seniors.

God bless America and help us all make her better!

Chapter 14 #4 Eliminate All Student Debt!!!

Student debt is huge

In 2018, the total amount of student debt outstanding was $1.48 Trillion. More and more young adults simply cannot repay their loans; so they are forced to default. Most are looking for relief but do not want to put the rest of America on the hook for an education that went bad for them. Universities and colleges take no blame, though most of us see them as the real perpetrators.

If Academia admitted they lied to the freshman, then maybe everybody today owing the national government for a student-loan package that committed kids to pay and pay and pay and pay and gain nothing, would be asking Academia to pony up a few bucks to solve the debt crisis. If anybody is at fault besides the 17-year olds who took on the debt, it is those that sold them on going into debt—the colleges and universities of America.

Many of our friends have asked: "Why do our young people no longer matter?" Do they matter? To the Matt Cartwright and Bob Casey Jr. Congress, they do not matter at all.

We Americans live in an age when everybody seems to have a reason to pick on millennials. It happens this group owes most of the student debt in America. I am sure your average Bank Officer would not loan a "spoiled" millennial "ingrate" as much as a dollar today for a cup of coffee.

However, the same millennial just a few years previous, was able to get a hundred-thousand-dollar loan or more at a college or university even though their young face gave away the fact that the debtor had yet to finish with puberty.

I regret that is true and now many of our youngest citizens are stuck because they committed at 18 years of age and some even as young as seventeen. Should these young people have been entrusted with such huge loans? No matter how much you do not like the millennial generation, you intrinsically know the answer.

Whether millennials are deserving of the bad rap or not, they represent a lost generation of our society. For the sake of all of America, they need to be invited back in. We all have student loan debtors in our families – sons, daughters, nephews, nieces, even grandparents and parents when we consider cosigners.

We admire those who have been able to pay their own loan debt, but we acknowledge many in our own families who cannot even afford the interest. And, so they become leaches on society and as time passes, we see that they no longer have the will to participate in the loan game at all. Some even drop out of life.

I have proposed that John Chrin and Lou Barletta offer legislation when first elected to make sure we solve this nasty American problem. There have been many other debt reliefs in our history but none that could deliver such an immediate positive punch to so many actual Americans all at once.

The upside of wiping out all student debt immediately, would be overwhelming. There would be a joint humanitarian return and a major economic return far greater than any bailout in history. Let's consider it. OK? It is not unprecedented. Don't rule it out OK?

A Bailout is a Bailout?

Many of us remember bailouts of the past from 2007 onward. We had bank bailouts, auto company bailouts, TARP bailouts and many other unnamed bailouts. Did any of these bailouts help your family? Of course not. They helped government cronies and the sons and daughters of Americans were not on the crony list.

Bailout fever began right before Obama became President and continued. The President managed all of the money—trillions. He chose not to give a dime to help student loan debt but spared no expense showering the degenerate financial institutions that owned his candidacy with gold.

Mike Collins, a Forbes Magazine contributor whose expertise focuses on manufacturing and government policy (not the former beloved magistrate of Wilkes-Barre, PA, who shares the same name and who passed away in May 2000) had this to say:

"Most people think that the big bank bailout was the $700 billion that the treasury department used to save the banks during the financial crash in September of 2008. But this is a long way from the truth because the bailout [ten years later] is still ongoing".

"The Special Inspector General for TARP's summary of the bailout says that the total commitment of government is $16.8 trillion dollars with $4.6 trillion already paid out." FYI, that is three times the total amount of student debt owed today.

[The same banks are now larger and still "too big to fail." But the indebted students are small potatoes, not significant enough to care about. So, their loans must be repaid.]

"But it isn't just the government bailout money that tells the story of the bailout. This is a story about lies, cheating, and a multi-faceted corruption, which was often criminal."

Like most elements of his presidency, Obama made the situation worse when he commandeered the student loan program from Sallie Mae and other lenders. The government now pulls in more than $50 billion a year from charging usury level interest rates to student borrowers. The Obama Student Loan Company charges 6.8% as student interest rates.

The CBO estimates that the interest rate on these loans should quickly be reduced from 6.8 percent to 5.3 percent if

Obama had not earmarked the profit from the backs of students to subsidize Obamacare.

Not only were millennials duped into huge college loans when they were so young that Clearasil was one of their major expenses, they were duped into believing Obama was in their corner.

Despite what a number of my conservative friends believe, your author believes these student victims deserve a break. Many are now adults. Many of the Americans stuck with huge cosign tabs are grandparents on Social Security. The government actually garnishes their SSR "checks" to pay back the Obama loans.

The federal government is putting up $16.8 trillion dollars as of 2018 to big banks, and other nameless faces receiving bailout dollars. We still do not know who is getting our money. But, we do know that at about $1.48 trillion of student debt in total in 2018, the crony friends of government are receiving ten times more of a benefit than our children. Granted many of our children do not need a dime but a much larger percentage need much more than a dime!

Students are still being victimized by usury after being preyed on as 17-year-olds by admissions counsellors for an all-but worthless college education leading to no job. If given the choice would you be helping the big banks or would you ask the government to help our own kids?

What do the people think about Student Debt?

Four in ten Americans believe that President Trump's administration should forgive all federal student debt in order to help stimulate the economy, according to a reasonably new survey revealed in 2017. As time goes by as more Americans realize we are excluding a full generation of Americans in our economy, this number will increase from a simple majority to an overwhelming endorsement of wiping out this scurrilous unfair debt as soon as possible.

We should bring these 48 million students back into the American way of life as soon as possible.

As we indicated at the beginning of this chapter, the largest share of blame for the student debt crisis lies with the promises made by over-zealous admissions counsellors who convinced immature adolescents to accept a new paradigm about growing up in America. Big bully adults told them it is OK at 18 or 17 or perhaps even 16, to sign up for $100,000 loans.

No American can want a full generation of other Americans to be left behind in the Trump economy. We need this debt eradicated now and we need to install safeguards so that young kids who think that they can handle anything, do not have to learn that they actually cannot by experiencing this tragic lesson. Without some help from other Americans, it is hopeless.

According to MoneyTips.com, attitudes have changed from a time when Americans thought college students should be punished for making bad choices to today, when we need 48 million new spenders in our economy. Can you imagine if they were all unleashed at the same time?

They would be unleashed into a world of productivity if no longer burdened with this massive debt. Many of us know first-hand the consequences of this debt burden. Though millennials may not be the most gracious in asking for help, they are Americans, not DACA immigrants, and they need our help now. Even if your child got through himself or herself, without any help, could you dare say no?

Do you want these young people to be poor all of their lives? Are you mad at them because they cannot pay back their loan but not be upset with others who use the bankruptcy courts or the welfare system to handle their debt? Think about the answer, please?

The raw economic fact, regardless of your philosophical preference is that spenders with the greatest potential to spend today are not spending at all in real numbers because of student debt. They are not getting married. They are not having families and they are not buying homes. We must solve this scourge on our country so that this generation can produce other generations of reasonably wealthy regular Americans.

I have friends who say "my Johnnie and my Elsie had to pay it all off and they did...those lazy louts should just cough it up!" As a country, the US has not ever had to vote to permit the poor to starve because somebody paid something more or less than somebody else. We should not start now.

Just remember that the children of Americans, our children are not MS-13 members in disguise; they are our kids— American kids. They were snookered to join academia for what they were deceived into believing was an indispensable college degree by depraved loan sharks. Let's give them a full chance to recover.

After what they went through, why not another chance? It costs a university nothing when their students with huge loans fail. Please let that sink in. Should they also take a stake at helping bring these students that they simply cast away, back as productive human beings?

Let me review the plight of young American college attendees and graduates. Barely out of adolescence, these young Americans were wheedled into commitments based on fraudulent promises by admissions counselors and financial institutions.

It was unfair to pit experienced loan sharks against adolescent teenagers. The students were further damned by a paid-for Congress, whose lobbyists insisted that these select few, with student debt, distinct from all of the others in debt in America, had no opportunity for any relief in the bankruptcy courts.

Non-college graduates with a trillion dollars in credit card debt are still able to obtain full relief from the courts. Why did Congress exclude these former teenagers, who clearly have been the biggest victims of loan-shark organized racketeering ever seen in America? Why?

I have asked John Chrin and Lou Barletta to take the following brief pledge to help us.

I, <u>John Chrin</u>, [I, <u>Lou Barletta</u>] am pledging today to solve this student debt problem as soon as I can. I am ready to take action by working to eliminate all student debt.

I hope you all agree. Let's help these young Americans before they are lost forever.

Young teenagers were told all through high school that the best ticket for a successful life is a college education. Is this true today? Their salaries often lag behind even those of non-college educated professionals such as plumbers, electricians, computer repair personnel, operating engineers, and more. Worse than that, they do not get jobs in their majors because most of the jobs are taken by those graduates from other countries with special visas who overstay.

Because of their reliance on these deliberately false misrepresentations, each of these young people now owe an approximate average of $50,000 in student debt while their admissions counsellors and loan sharks revel in riches, in their Mercedes, BMW's, and third vacation home on the lake.

Unscrupulous malefactors with self-interest-filled agendas persuaded America's teenagers, many so young they still had Acne vulgaris, to dig themselves huge financial holes with no escape. Universities are at least partly responsible for their unfulfilled promises. Don't you think?

We must also consider what liability they may share in compensating this lost generation where one out of six student borrowers must default today, a figure that only has increased with time.

Removing this debt may not fully compensate for the bad hand they were dealt, but its consequent increase in economic activity will benefit all of us. It will boost the US economy beyond expectations. We are already giving bailouts of over $16 trillion to obscenely rich people in corporate shadows. Who says we cannot help our American progeny even if they are millennials?

Right now, we need a mere 10% of that number to pay for the write-off of student debt without hurting taxpayers and without putting any banks under. The savings over three years, for example from the resident visa program alone pays off the entire student debt that exists today. Why support illegal aliens when we can help Americans?

One last point. It helps to recall that President Obama increased the National Debt by $9.1 Trillion in just eight years, hoping to assure that illegal aliens had all the resources they needed to take as many American jobs as they could. Name me a better reason?

This is six times the amount of debt owed by young Americans. Obama nearly doubled our debt. And what do we have to show for that? For a typical college student in the Obama years, the answer is frankly... nothing. By contrast, debt relief for our young Americans will be visibly positive in its impact.

So, let's say Congress wipes out all student debt because it is the fair thing to do. How do we prevent this from ever happening again? For this, I thank my great friend, Dennis Grimes whose solution combines some skin in the game for Academic Institutions to the mix and thus assures that no student will ever carry debt unless the student is successful with a job in their field of study. I will ask John Chrin and Lou Barletta to sponsor the Grimes legislation. Here is how the new loan system designed by Dennis Grimes would work.

Nobody gets a loan unless the college or university agrees to take all of the risk of the loan. If the student is successful, she or he will pay very reasonable amounts on a monthly basis. If the student is jobless, since the university vouched for the student, the school will owe all of the debt.

Academic institutions are smart. They will stop lending quickly to students with very little prospects of being able to pay the loan back. If students do not maintain acceptable averages, they will be expelled, and the university will pay their balance. If the same student wants to go to college in the future, it will be cash only. What do you think?

A Rigged System

You and I are confident that President Trump would re-enfranchise America's youngest generation of adults. by eradicating student debt and paying the balance via savings no longer spent subsidizing illegal immigrants.

In his own words, regarding recent graduates: "They go, and they work, and they take loans, and they're borrowed up, and they can't breathe, and they get through college and the worst thing is, they go through that whole process and they don't have any job." Trump has it right. He sees how this rigged system has snuffed out the optimism of a bright generation that now gives way to cynicism and despair.

I am expecting that John Chrin and Lou Barletta already know how important this is. When Chrin replaces Cartwright and becomes our Representative and Barletta replaces Casey and becomes our US Senator, I would expect that they would help enact the legislation that eradicates all Student Debt, effective immediately.

Thank you, John Chrin, and Lou Barletta for your consideration.

The people realize that none of this will happen until they can get John Chrin elected as District 8 Representative to Congress and they can get Lou Barletta elected as US Senator from Pennsylvania. Then, these measures can be brought up to the legislature of the US and will become well-known to the conservative press, seniors and millennials. Any American saddled with the direct result of the abuse of our legislators should not be quiet in these important matters.

God Bless America!

Other Books by Brian Kelly: (amazon.com, and Kindle)

Millennials Say America Was "Never That Great": Too many pleased days of political chumps not over!
White People Are Bad! Bad! Bad! In 2018, too many people find race as a non-equalizer.
It's Time for The John Doe Party… Don't you think? By By Elephants.
Great Players in Florida Gators Football… Tim Tebow and a ton of other great players
Great Coaches in Florida Gators Football… The best coaches in Gator history.
The Constitution by Hamilton, Jefferson, Madison, et al. The Real Constitution
The Constitution Companion. Will help you learn and understand the Constitution
Great Coaches in Clemson Football The best Clemson Coaches right to Dabo Swinney
Great Players in Clemson Football The best Clemson players in history
Winning Back America. America's been stolen and can be won back completely
The Founding of America… Great book to pick up a lot of great facts
Defeating America's Career Politicians. The scoundrels need to go.
Midnight Mass by Jack Lammers… You remember what it was like Great story
The Bike by Jack Lammers… Great heartwarming Story by Jack
Wipe Out All Student Loan Debt--Now! Watch the economy go boom!
No Free Lunch Pay Back Welfare! Why not pay it back?
Deport All Millennials Now!!! Why they deserve to be deported and/or saved
DELETE the EPA, Please! The worst decisions to hurt America
Taxation Without Representation 4th Edition Should we throw the TEA overboard again?
Four Great Political Essays by Thomas Dawson
Top Ten Political Books for 2018… Cliffnotes Version of 10 Political Books
Top Six Patriotic Books for 2018… Cliffnotes version of 6 Patriotic Boosk
Why Trump Got Elected!.. It's great to hear about a great milestone in America!
The Day the Free Press Died. Corrupt Press Lives on!
Solved (Immigration) The best solutions for 2018
Solved II (Obamacare, Social Security, Student Debt) Check it out; They're solved.
Great Moments in Pittsburgh Steelers Football… Six Super Bowls and more.
Great Players in Pittsburgh Steelers Football ,,,Chuck Noll, Bill Cowher, Mike Tomin, etc.
Great Coaches in New England Patriots Football,,, Bill Belichick the one and only plus others
Great Players in New England Patriots Football… Tom Brady, Drew Bledsoe et al.
Great Coaches in Philadelphia Eagles Football..Andy Reid, Doug Pederson & Lots more
Great Players in Philadelphia Eagles Football Great players such as Sonny Jurgenson
Great Coaches in Syracuse Football All the greats including Ben Schwartzwalder
Great Players in Syracuse Football. Highlights best players such as Jim Brown & Donovan McNabb
Millennials are People Too !!! Give US millennials help to live American Dream
Brian Kelly for the United States Senate from PA: Fresh Face for US Senate
The Candidate's Bible. Don't pray for your campaign without this bible
Rush Limbaugh's Platform for Americans… Rush will love it
Sean Hannity's Platform for Americans… Sean will love it
Donald Trump's New Platform for Americans. Make Trump unbeatable in 2020
Tariffs Are Good for America! One of the best tools a president can have
Great Coaches in Pittsburgh Steelers Football Sixteen of the best coaches ever to coach in pro football.
Great Moments in New England Patriots Football Great football moments from Boston to New England
Great Moments in Philadelphia Eagles Football. The best from the Eagles from the beginning of football.
Great Moments in Syracuse Football The great moments, coaches & players in Syracuse Football
Boost Social Security Now! Hey Buddy Can You Spare a Dime?
The Birth of American Football. From the first college game in 1869 to the last Super Bowl
Obamacare: A One-Line Repeal Congress must get this done.
A Wilkes-Barre Christmas Story A wonderful town makes Christmas all the better
A Boy, A Bike, A Train, and a Christmas Miracle A Christmas story that will melt your heart
Pay-to-Go America-First Immigration Fix
Legalizing Illegal Aliens Via Resident Visas Americans-first plan saves $Trillions. Learn how!
60 Million Illegal Aliens in America!!! A simple, America-first solution.
The Bill of Rights By Founder James Madison Refresh *your knowledge of the specific rights for all*
Great Players in Army Football Great Army Football played by great players..
Great Coaches in Army Football Army's coaches are all great.
Great Moments in Army Football Army Football at its best.
Great Moments in Florida Gators Football Gators Football from the start. This is the book.
Great Moments in Clemson Football CU Football at its best. This is the book.
Great Moments in Florida Gators Football Gators Football from the start. This is the book.

The Constitution Companion. A Guide to Reading and Comprehending the Constitution
The Constitution by Hamilton, Jefferson, & Madison – Big type and in English
PATERNO: The Dark Days After Win # 409. Sky began to fall within days of win # 409.
JoePa 409 Victories: Say No More! Winningest Division I-A football coach ever
American College Football: The Beginning From before day one football was played.
Great Coaches in Alabama Football Challenging the coaches of every other program!
Great Coaches in Penn State Football the Best Coaches in PSU's football program
Great Players in Penn State Football The best players in PSU's football program
Great Players in Notre Dame Football The best players in ND's football program
Great Coaches in Notre Dame Football The best coaches in any football program
Great Players in Alabama Football from Quarterbacks to offensive Linemen Greats!
Great Moments in Alabama Football AU Football from the start. This is the book.
Great Moments in Penn State Football PSU Football, start--games, coaches, players,
Great Moments in Notre Dame Football ND Football, start, games, coaches, players
Cross Country with the Parents A great trip from East Coast to West with the kids
Seniors, Social Security & the Minimum Wage. Things seniors need to know.
How to Write Your First Book and Publish It with CreateSpace
The US Immigration Fix--It's all in here. Finally, an answer.
I had a Dream IBM Could be #1 Again The title is self-explanatory
WineDiets.Com Presents The Wine Diet Learn how to lose weight while having fun.
Wilkes-Barre, PA; Return to Glory Wilkes-Barre City's return to glory
Geoffrey Parsons' Epoch... The Land of Fair Play Better than the original.
The Bill of Rights 4 Dummmies! This is the best book to learn about your rights.
Sol Bloom's Epoch ...Story of the Constitution The best book to learn the Constitution
America 4 Dummmies! All Americans should read to learn about this great country.
The Electoral College 4 Dummmies! How does it really work?
The All-Everything Machine Story about IBM's finest computer server.
ThankYou IBM! This book explains how IBM was beaten in the computer marketplace by neophytes

Amazon.com/author/brianwkelly
Brian W. Kelly has written 177 books. Thank you for buying this one.